Library Instruction

Library Instruction

A Peer Tutoring Model

Susan Deese-Roberts, Ph.D.
Associate Professor
University of New Mexico General Library
Albuquerque, New Mexico

Kathleen Keating
Associate Professor
University of New Mexico General Library
Albuquerque, New Mexico

2000
Libraries Unlimited, Inc.
Englewood, Colorado

*To the University of New Mexico students
who have contributed to the Library Instruction Tutor Program through their input
and their participation as tutors and tutees.*

To Chuck Roberts and George Farr, the husbands who supported and endured.

Libraries Unlimited, Inc.
P.O. Box 6633
Englewood, CO 80155-6633
1-800-237-6124
www.lu.com

Library of Congress Cataloging-in-Publication Data

Deese-Roberts, Susan, 1953-
 Library instruction : a peer tutoring model / Susan Deese-Roberts, Kathleen Keating.
  p. cm.
 Includes bibliographical references and index.
 ISBN 1-56308-652-2 (pbk.)
  1. Library orientation for college students--United States. 2. Peer-group tutoring of
students--United States. I. Keating, Kathleen, 1958- II. Title.

Z711.2 .D44 2000
027.6′2--dc21
                                                                    00-055850

Contents

Acknowledgments

The authors thank the following groups and individuals for their roles in establishing the Library Instruction Tutoring Program at the University of New Mexico General Library (UNMGL). The pilot project and on-going program would not have succeeded without their collaborative efforts, support, and hard work. Former colleague Linda St. Clair recognized the efficacy and value of a library instruction role for peer tutors. Her ideas and support were inspirational and invaluable. General Library Dean Robert Migneault provided an environment of support and innovation for the creation of the program. The UNMGL faculty and staff participated in providing valuable input into the tutor training curriculum and tutoring session content. Without the participation of these individuals in establishing the fundamental elements, the authors alone could not have created such a broad-based, professionally designed library instruction tutor training curriculum. The Center for Academic Program Support (CAPS) staff, especially Mary Ellen Kurucz and Karen Olson, provided the collaboration needed for successful implementation of the Library Instruction Tutor Program. The CAPS infrastructure provided the instrument and standards for tutor hiring, training, scheduling, and evaluation. Thanks to the College Reading and Learning Association for permission to reprint their International Tutor Training Certification Program guidelines and list of certified programs. A special thanks to Pauline Heffern, Education Programs and Services (EPS) Administrative Assistant, for allowing the authors to work together with few interruptions, and to all EPS faculty and staff members for their support during the authors' sabbaticals and research leave. And most important, a special recognition to the tutors who participated in the pilot project and first provided library instruction tutoring services to UNM students—Meridith Alvarez, Hanaa Benhalim, Russell Turek, and Jennifer Ingram. Their humor, flexibility, patience, and dedication to learning and imparting library research skills to students were the heart and success of the program.

Introduction

This book proposes the application of peer tutoring to library instruction, primarily in the academic library setting. New technologies are changing the ways in which library users access information. Reference and instruction librarians are experiencing a dramatic increase in questions about using electronic resources, selecting and manipulating appropriate databases, using the World Wide Web, and evaluating the information found. New forms of access have created the need for a new level of service at reference desks and within instruction programs.

Library instruction peer tutoring services do not replace traditional reference and instruction services, but add a new approach. This new level of instruction includes teaching concepts that allow library users to be independent. Users are able to provide creative solutions to research problems when they are able to confront information needs with knowledge of information. Many library users are no longer in the library. A computer and modem can provide access to on-line catalogs, the Web, and other networked databases such as those residing on CD-ROMs. Many reference and instruction programs are overwhelmed by increasing demands for assistance and are seeking new solutions.

Using student peers to teach introductory library skills is a new application of a proven learning technique. Peer tutors are used on many campuses to assist students with basic skill development in areas such as writing and critical reading; with study strategy development including test taking, note taking, and time management skills; and/or with content mastery in specific courses. We propose that using peer tutors to provide library instruction is an effective and easy solution to the increasing demand for instruction services.

The primary audience for this book includes reference and instruction librarians in academic libraries. A secondary audience includes directors of learning assistance centers. This book provides information that can help librarians and learning assistance professionals collaborate in offering tutorial services for library instruction.

Chapter 1 provides a brief historical view of library instruction and current trends that make peer tutoring a possible form of library service. Chapter 2 describes peer tutoring as currently practiced in higher education. Chapters 3 and 4 provide principles and guidelines for establishing peer tutoring programs with a focus on library instruction tutoring. Chapters 5 and 6 include the concepts for developing a tutor training program and a practical model for a library instruction tutoring program. Chapter 7 is composed of an analysis of our experience at the UNMGL, including program improvements and future plans. Chapter 8 explores the application of library instruction peer tutoring model to K–12 education. The appendices contain training materials and selected peer tutoring resources.

Chapter 1

Library Instruction Overview

The recent introduction of new information technologies into academic libraries renewed interest in library instruction programs. A historical review of the field of library instruction reveals that current practices combine the old with the new. Ideas more than 100 years old and new roles for librarians are helping to form current directions in academic library instruction programs. Tucker (1984) outlined a historical timeframe delineating three distinct instruction movements: from 1870 to 1930, the Professor of Bibliography Movement; from 1930 to 1970, the Library–College Movement; and from 1970 to present, the Information Literacy Movement. A fourth area presented focuses on trends for the future. The following review provides a library context for exploring peer tutoring of library strategies as a viable library instruction service.

1870 TO 1930: THE PROFESSOR OF BIBLIOGRAPHY MOVEMENT

After the Civil War, higher education was changed by the introduction and rapid growth of graduate-level degree programs and by the establishment of land-grant institutions. The British model of classical and religious curriculum was changed to include technical and professional programs. Original research became a product of academic enterprise, and the seminar method of instruction was introduced. Students began making presentations in class and were able for the first time to design individual programs of study. Teaching faculty were becoming more specialized and less able to work with students in a variety of disciplines.

As colleges and universities changed, so did the role of the library and librarians at these institutions. Research collections were developed and collection sizes grew rapidly. The Dewey Decimal Classification System was published in 1876. The American Library Association was founded that same year and the first issue of *American Library Journal* was published. The first library school was established in 1887 at Columbia College (Wiegand 1996). Library instruction as a library service was advocated and library instruction courses were offered.

Many of the early academic librarians were teaching faculty assigned at least part-time to the library. Often generalists in discipline, they were interested in teaching students the skills needed to independently explore library resources. Otis Hall Robinson, librarian at the University of Rochester from 1868 until 1889, was one such faculty member. Robinson (1880) described the changes in libraries by noting:

> The idea that a college librarian may serve the classes as an instructor quite as successfully as the professor of Latin or of mathematics is beginning to take root. It is beginning to be understood also that teachers can make an important use of the library in giving their regular instruction. In many places the libraries are become so large that careful attention must be given by readers to selection. . . . The time is passing also when the chief duty of a librarian was to collect books and preserve them. How to get them used most extensively, most intelligently, and at the same time carefully, is becoming his chief concern (19).

Justin Winsor, head of the Harvard University Library from 1877 to 1897, is another professor used to exemplify this period of library instruction history. Winsor (1894) advocated a central role for libraries and librarians in the teaching mission of the university.

> The system has gone a step further in the creation of classroom libraries, close at hand in the hour of instruction, and ten or a dozen of these supplemental collections show from a few score to a few thousand volumes each. All this has conduced to an enormous increase in the use of books, and our statistics reveal that a very small proportion of the students are not frequenters of the library.
>
> Nor is this all, which is, in these latter days, done to facilitate the use of the books. Systematic instruction in bibliographical research keeps in the van of every subject a cloud of skirmishers, who bring in title after title for the consideration of the library authorities. Thus, the whole system becomes a practical endowment of research, the library becomes a central agency in college work (374).

Azariah Root, director of the Oberlin College Library from 1887 to 1927, devised a three-course program of library instruction. The courses were not designed for a library school curriculum, but rather for the regular university curriculum.

Root had designed a step-by-step process for the education of students interested in library instruction. It was a curriculum which demanded from the student a high quality of research, particularly on the advanced levels. The final step in this process reflected a criterion much more consistent with the graduate level than the undergraduate, demonstrating not only Root's high academic standards, but his prescience in demanding graduate-level performance (Rubin 1977, 257).

These early academic librarians connected the library to the central mission of the university by involving librarians in the teaching functions of the faculty and by helping students become independent library users. These librarians were prepared to accept the role of providing general education to students. The work, though, of Winsor, Robinson, Root, and others did not result in a long-lasting establishment of library instruction in academic libraries or the establishment of the academic library in a central role of universities.

Several factors contributed to changes within academic libraries leading toward programs other than library instruction. Tremendous increases in the size of collections required that more emphasis be placed on the technical aspects of accessing information. Establishing reference services allowed a shift from instructing in library use to providing answers to questions on an ad hoc basis. During this time, the library profession as a whole experienced a general decline. Ironically, the establishment of library schools resulted in more librarians as technicians and fewer librarians interested in engaging in scholarship and college curriculum. Hopkins (1982) described this period by noting:

Most of the new library graduates were neither the intellectual nor social equals of academic faculty. BI [bibliographic instruction] of the sort developed by Winsor and Root could not be routinized or divorced from familiarity with the curriculum and research methods, and it is unlikely that the new breed of librarians would be have attempted it. . . . To the average library school graduate, the role of reference librarian must have been much more congenial than any attempt to emulate Justin Winsor as professor of bibliography (194).

1930 TO 1970: THE LIBRARY–COLLEGE MOVEMENT

During the 1930s, a new framework for academic librarianship, the library–college, was proposed. This framework emphasized the equality of librarians and faculty and called on both to create partnerships for new ways of student learning. The library–college model was explored both before and after World War II.

Louis Shores proposed the library–college during the mid-1930s. He envisioned

> a teaching and learning situation for students that moved most educational experiences from the classroom to the library. As envisioned, the library–college presupposed abolition of regular class attendance in favor of studying in the library, merging all physical facilities into a single library complex, peer instruction of beginning undergraduates by upper-class students, integration of librarians and professors into a single teaching staff and a liberal arts curriculum that focused on techniques of problem solving within a liberal arts curriculum. He saw a true partnership between faculty and librarians (Coughlin and Gertzog 1992, 333).

Patricia Knapp's (1966) application of the library–college concept at Monteith College in the early 1960s was an experiment in fully integrating library instruction into the educational curriculum.

> Our original notion that the ineffectiveness of traditional library instruction is due to its isolation from "content" courses was reinforced by our experience with the pilot project. But we are no longer content with the simple goal of getting the library somehow or other built into such courses. The relationship is more complicated than we thought. If it is to be effective, the library program must be not merely presented in the context of "content" courses, but truly consistent in goals and methods, in tone and style, with the overall education program in which it occurs (88).

The project involved creating sequential library assignments that were focused on information problem solving and were integrated into the university curriculum. Unfortunately, the Monteith experiment failed in large part because the faculty members were unwilling to fully collaborate with the librarians.

The library–college framework for instruction was adopted by very few academic institutions and had seemingly little immediate influence on academic libraries. However, ideas from the period, especially those related to collaboration between librarians and faculty and integration of library assignments into the curriculum, are seen in later library innovations. Also, even though these library–college efforts were not successful at the time, Farber (1995) recognized that the "emphasis on librarians as teachers did get a number of librarians to think about that role, and it provided a forum for those who became interested in pursuing the issue in more practical ways" (26). Discussions of librarians as teachers will undoubtedly continue into the new millennium.

After World War II, access to higher education was made available to larger numbers of Americans than ever before. Admissions standards based on student merit rather than ability to pay became the symbol of a new philosophy of access to higher education. The GI Bill provided the financial means to attend college for thousands of men and women who otherwise might have considered a college education unaffordable. Government emphasis on science and technology research brought additional federal funds to higher education. Funds became available for books to support research, and the size of academic libraries grew. Trained librarians were in short supply, and the emphasis of training was on technical expertise.

The librarian as a technical expert rather than an educator was once again seen as the core of librarianship. "Through the 1950s library instruction—usually routine or merely remedial where it was offered at all—was almost completely eclipsed by developments in technical services, which were at once more interesting and more advantageous for the professionalization of librarianship" (Hopkins 1982, 195).

Again, as they had in the late 1800s, academic libraries responded to new resources with

> rapid collection growth and with new techniques of organization and retrieval. Consequently, in the 1960s, as in the 1880s, there was a severe shortage of trained librarians. The library school had been upgrading gradually and the fifth-year master's degree had by this time become standard; now the school began offering courses in documentation and computer applications. Job mobility and salaries improved, and librarians began to gain some recognition as technical experts (Hopkins 1982, 195).

Although science and technology had a great influence on the specialization of higher education curriculum and on the training of academic librarians, powerful social forces also influenced higher education during the 1960s. Civil rights, the widespread use of recreational drugs, opposition to the Vietnam War, and the rapid democratization of access to higher education created a mood of rebellion on and off college and university campuses. On campus, student groups demanded new programs that focused on the study of women and minorities. Students demanded more options for creating individualized programs of study. Undergraduate education was re-examined in terms of these demands and because large numbers of students were poorly prepared for college study. These forces, which also included rapid increases in enrollments, shaped the form of library instruction.

In the public colleges and universities especially, ad hoc
reference service was not adequate to the needs of increasing numbers of students who lacked basic library competence but who were nevertheless expected to cope with a
bibliographic apparatus geared to graduate students and
faculty. In this situation, library instruction focused on general access skills and on use of the more technical bibliographic tools (Hopkins 1982, 196).

Social and political forces created significant changes in higher education during the library–college movement. The result was less emphasis on library instruction and greater emphasis on technology and growth. Instruction efforts
were also eclipsed by reference services. The library–college concept was not
successfully implemented in total, but many of the concepts, such as closer
work with teaching faculty and library responsibility for general education, did
pave the way for coming innovations in instruction.

1970 TO THE 1990S: THE INFORMATION LITERACY MOVEMENT

Although the latter part of the nineteenth century saw the development
of American librarianship as a profession through the establishment of library
associations and periodicals, the latter twentieth century saw the establishment
of professional library instruction organizations and periodicals. The Bibliographic Instruction Section of the Association of College and Research Libraries
and the Library Instruction Round Table of the American Library Association
were founded. *Research Strategies*, a periodical devoted exclusively to library instruction, was first published in 1983. A clearinghouse for library instruction, the
Library Orientation–Instruction Exchange (LOEX), was established in 1972 and
has since sponsored more than 20 annual conferences.

A survey LOEX conducted in December 1979 painted a picture of library instruction activities at 830 libraries (Kirkendall 1980). When compared
to a similar survey of 193 libraries in 1973, it was found that some activities,
such as preparation of detailed bibliographies and conducted tours, declined
during the period. Other areas, however, expanded: computer-assisted instruction; credit courses; self-paced, programmed workbooks and exercises; required library units in composition and communication courses; audiovisual
tools at point of use; pretests and attitude surveys; database searching instruction; and subject-related instruction.

The 1979 survey was replicated in 1987 (Mensching 1989). At that
time, 834 libraries responded. The availability or use of credit courses, term
paper clinics, audiotapes, printed handbooks, and instruction services to
groups other than faculty or students declined between 1979 and 1987. Point-
of-use instruction (especially in videotape and print), individualized instruction, and computer-assisted instruction showed significant increases. Also,

the percentage of libraries reporting that some form of bibliographic instruction or library-use competency was required rose from 24 percent in 1979 to 65 percent in 1987. The most popular methods of required instruction were course-related lectures or tours, course-related exercises, workbook completion, and library credit courses.

Course-related instruction was the hallmark of library instruction programs during the 1970s and 1980s. The most common structure of course-related instruction was the presentation by a librarian during a regular course time period. These sessions often included a figurative or literal tour of the library and descriptions and displays of reference materials related to the course subject. The influence of the library–college movement was seen in these instruction partnerships between librarians and teaching faculty.

During the 1980s, information technology began to have a significant impact on libraries, librarians, and higher education in general. Even though automation was not new to libraries, the information technologies of the 1980s accelerated changes within academic libraries by providing users direct access to more and larger information databases. Database searching was no longer an activity undertaken almost exclusively by librarians; direct access to a variety of electronic databases was now available to students and faculty. As specialized training became necessary for this end-user searching, librarians reexamined instruction programs. They became concerned about teaching students the skills needed to be successful in the Information Age—to be information literate. Learning about the on-line catalog system, for example, was no longer an adequate objective of an instruction program. The library's on-line catalog software might change several times during a student's attendance at the university and was quickly becoming only one of many electronic resources readily available to library users. Hardware and software changes were taking place so rapidly that librarians had trouble maintaining previous levels of expertise, much less helping students attain and maintain levels of expertise. Of additional concern was the fact that many teaching faculty needed help in using electronic information. Many faculty members were no longer able to assist students with library use; faculty needed to participate in instruction programs as students themselves.

Behrens (1994) reported that Paul Zurkowski, then president of the Information Industry Association (IIA), was the first to use the concept of information literacy. In a proposal to the National Commission on Libraries and Information Science, Zurkowski (1974) described information literates and illiterates:

> People trained in the application of information resources to their work can be called information literates. They have learned techniques and skills for utilizing the wide range of information tools as well as primary sources in molding information-solutions to their problems.
>
> The individuals in the remaining portion of the population, while literate in the sense that they can read and

> write, do not have a measure for the value of information,
> do not have an ability to mold information to their needs,
> and realistically must be considered information illiterates
> (6).

In addition, he declared that five out of six residents of the United States were information illiterate.

Information literacy was tied to the advent of the Information Age. Futurists predicted a global transition from the modern industrial age to a new age of information.

> The Information Age is upon us. This third and arguably
> most transformational of the industrial/technological revo-
> lutions that have taken us from farm, to factory, to elec-
> tronic workplace, is being driven by an acceleration of
> powerful electronic microprocessors. A partial listing of
> these technological innovations would include: microcom-
> puters, cable TV, electronic publishing, fiber optics, satel-
> lite communications, videotext, on-line database searching,
> high-density CD-ROM storage, and robotics. Whether or
> not we have yet incorporated these innovations into the
> conduct of our daily activities, most of us have acquired at
> least a passing awareness of what they might do for us.
> What they all do best, of course, is process, store, retrieve,
> and transmit huge amounts of information at extremely
> high speeds (Demo 1986, 1).

Numerous definitions of information literacy have emerged during the past two decades. In 1979, five years after Zurkowski's definition was first pre-sented, the IIA issued a revision of the definition that excluded a reference to workplace application. The revised definition defined an information literate as "a person who knows the techniques and skills for using information tools in molding solutions to problems" (Garfield 1979, 210). Also in 1979, Taylor proposed that information literacy would include the elements of (1) finding solutions to most problems through information acquisition, (2) acknowledg-ing that a requisite of information literacy is knowing a variety of information resources, (3) understanding that the process of informing is continual as well as occasional, and (4) recognizing that there are strategies of information ac-quisition. These definitions of the 1970s introduced requisites for information literacy, but it was not until the late 1980s that specific information literacy skills and knowledge were identified.

In the 1980s, new information technologies were increasingly ap-parent not only in libraries and the workplace but also in homes. Computers were replacing typewriters and calculators in the office and at home. New-generation on-line catalogs were introduced in many libraries. VCRs, cable television, CD-ROMs, and other information tools were widely available.

Definitions of information literacy in the early 1980s acknowledged the relationship between information literacy and the use of computers. Horton (1983) distinguished information literacy from computer literacy by stating: "Information literacy, then, as opposed to computer literacy, means raising the levels of awareness of individuals and enterprises to the knowledge explosion, and how machine-aided handling systems can help to identify, access, and obtain data, documents and literature needed for problem-solving and decision-making" (16).

Librarians urged caution at the idea that exposure to computers and other information tools would simply lead to information literacy. Demo (1986) was concerned by the assumption that

> such literacy will rapidly follow the diffusion of machinery. The process by which people become information literate is thus often seen as a spontaneous by-product of their exposure to information and the instruments of its access and delivery. . . . There is considerable evidence to suggest that instead of lowering barriers to the acquisition of information skills needed to access information in personally and socially relevant ways they are instead creating new obstacles to the attainment of information literacy for many (8, 9).

He encouraged exploration of the complexities of the concept and called for delineation of specific information competencies. He suggested that academic librarians should provide the leadership in defining and forming information literacy programs.

One academic library program that received attention during the 1980s was the information literacy program developed at the Auraria Library on the Denver campus of the University of Colorado. The library serves a community college, a four-year college, and a university. The program was based on a working definition of information literacy that incorporated more specific skills than previous definitions. According to the working definition (Breivik 1985), information literacy is (1) an integrated set of skills (research strategy and evaluation) and knowledge of tools and resources; (2) developed through acquisition of persistence, attention to detail and caution in accepting printed word and single sources; (3) time and labor intensive; (4) driven by need to solve a problem; and (5) distinct from but related to literacy and computer literacy. Information literacy is not (1) only the knowledge of resources; (2) solely dependent on the library; and (3) limited to finding information.

The American Library Association created The Presidential Committee on Information Literacy in 1987 and the committee report in 1989 provided what is now the most commonly used definition of an information literate person.

> To be information literate, a person must be able to recognize when information is needed and have the ability to locate, evaluate, and use effectively the needed information. . . . Ultimately, information literate people are those who have learned how to learn. They know how to learn because they know how knowledge is organized, how to find information, and how to use information in such a way that others can learn from them. They are people prepared for lifelong learning, because they can always find the information needed for any task or decision at hand (1).

The committee proposed a new model for learning that emphasized resource-based learning rather than packaged learning through textbooks, workbooks, and lectures. Libraries as a collection and access point for a variety of information resources would be central to this new process. The committee's report suggested specific activities for students as they participate in this new learning process and become information literate: "Knowing when they have a need for information, identifying information needed to address a given problem or issue, finding needed information, evaluating the information, organizing the information, using the information effectively to address the problem or issue at hand" (7).

While information and library professionals were refining definitions of information literacy during the 1980s, a national debate concerning educational reform was taking place. Unfortunately, librarians and libraries were often excluded as key elements in the reform process. The information literacy movement with its implications for restructuring the learning process was one avenue for librarians to become important participants in the reform process. Behrens (1994) suggested that information literacy goals were directly tied to the educational reform process. "The adoption of the information literacy goal was the library profession's response to having its role essentially ignored or overlooked in the educational reform process. Librarians now began paying attention to the connection between user education, information literacy, and lifelong learning" (313).

THE FUTURE: LIBRARIAN AS EDUCATOR

Information literacy and lifelong learning require librarians to become educators, to create learning environments in which the emphasis is on student learning and not simply on the teaching of skills. This aspect of the movement appears to be a major focus of the 1990s and beginning of the twenty-first century. Librarians no longer serve simply in partnerships with teaching faculty but must become educators themselves. Curriculum design, instructional models, conceptual frameworks, assessment and evaluation of teaching, and library school curriculum changes to include training librarians as teachers are some of the instruction-related topics appearing in library literature and on library conference programs. Student learning is becoming the assessment measure of higher education. The transition from teaching to learning is the current major challenge of postsecondary education. Lifelong learning is becoming the goal of education, supplanting the transmission of knowledge. Students must learn how to learn, not only for current needs, but also for future success. The need for learning to learn skills may be more apparent in libraries than in any other part of academic institutions. What students learned about using libraries just five years ago is mostly obsolete today.

The librarian as educator is not a new theme of the library instruction field. During the Professor of Bibliography Movement, librarians were educators, teaching faculty with assignments to the library. The focus of the library–college movement was to make the library the teaching college of the university. Social, political, and technological changes, however, turned the focus from librarians as educators to librarians as technical experts and technical instructors during these time periods. It was technology again that brought about enormous change in libraries and library instruction during the Information Literacy Movement. Currently, though, technology may bring emphasis to the educator role of librarians rather than to the technical expert role. Library users are becoming technical experts themselves by using information technology in their homes and offices. Technical expertise is no longer held primarily by library and information professionals, but has become widely available to the public. Education reform's emphasis on developing lifelong learning skills including research and critical thinking skills and on securing access to information technology places librarians in a key role as educators of the future.

Librarians have the opportunity to gain (or regain) a central academic role in the teaching, research, and service missions of the university. Rather than supporting these core institutional purposes, the library can now participate as a full partner. As student learning becomes the focus of the institution, the learning that occurs in the library can be seen as essential to the goal of developing lifelong learners. Technology allows for new interactions between student and teacher and between student and information. The growing field of distance education creates new roles for student and teacher and new paradigms for instruction. Libraries that continue to focus on collections and on storing and retrieving information will continue to compete for scarce resources; the result at most institutions is a decline in purchasing power and, therefore, a smaller collection of information. The library that focuses its mission solely on acquiring, storing, and retrieving information and materials will be relegated to the sidelines of the academic community.

The concept of the "teaching library" has been offered as a description of the library that is central to the university's mission.

> One major way in which the library can respond to the present challenges in higher education, maintain itself as a viable campus unit, and realize its potential as the symbolic

heart of the campus is to become a "teaching library." By the term teaching library, the authors refer to a library which is not only a support service for academic programs, but which is itself actively and directly involved in implementing the mission of higher education: teaching, research, and community service (Guskin, Stoffle, and Boisse 1979, 283).

Guskin and coauthors (1979) proposed bibliographic instruction, at elementary and advanced levels, as the essential program of the teaching library. They defined a comprehensive instruction program as having the following elements, in accordance with the 1977 Association of College and Research Libraries bibliographic instruction guidelines:

> (1) a general orientation to available facilities and resources, (2) the teaching of basic research skills and strategies, and (3) the teaching of the organization of the literature in various disciplines, as well as the basic reference tools in each discipline. In addition, the program should be characterized by (1) a written profile identifying the audiences for the instruction and their needs, (2) a written statement of instructional goals and objectives, and (3) a plan for evaluating the instruction program (285).

The Leavey Library at the University of Southern California represents the implementation of the teaching library concept. Deputy University Librarian Tompkins (1990) proposed five goals for the teaching library: (1) humanizing the use of technologies in learning; (2) providing a campus center for faculty and students where technology for collaboration is readily available; (3) providing a campus center for faculty and students using library resources locally and globally; (4) integrating traditional information sources with emerging learning and information technologies; and (5) offering training in information access and evaluation and the development of teaching materials. The vision for the library included

> (1) serving as a center for undergraduate intellectual life, (2) acting as a test bed for services and information technologies in the curriculum, and (3) being a concept and a place that transcends conventional notions of undergraduate education and that encourages interaction among student, faculty, and the world of ideas (Holmes-Wong et al. 1997, 75).

The concepts of the teaching library and the librarian as educator era are not designed to simply place the librarian in the traditional role of teaching faculty. Higher education is experiencing a shift in focus from teaching to learning. The teacher-centered classroom is being replaced with student-centered, outcomes-based approaches to teaching and learning. Barr and Tagg (1995) described this shift as a move from an "instruction model" of teaching and learning to a "learning model." The former aims to deliver instruction and transfer knowledge from faculty to students; the latter focuses on encouraging learning and student discovery and on constructing knowledge.

This paradigm shift also includes a change from the competitive classroom to a cooperative, collaborative environment inside and outside the classroom. The role of the faculty in the traditional instructional model is that of lecturer and expert. In the learning model, the role of the faculty is to work in partnership with students to design appropriate learning methods and environments. In the learning model, student learning is assessed through external outcomes measures rather than solely through faculty assigned grades (as in the instructional model). The learning model assumes that students are active learners with a teacher as a facilitator or guide or without anyone in the formal teacher role; the instructional model is based on passive students reacting to teacher stimulation.

Librarians must become familiar with learning theories and related teaching strategies that support the learning model. Active learning techniques incorporate powerful learning and teaching strategies into curriculums. These strategies are designed to engage learners by using a variety of learning modalities and recognizing differences in learning styles. The techniques are usually quite simple but the purposeful application of the techniques fosters greater student learning.

> One simple method is small group discussion, in which students discuss a problem or issue in a small group, record their conclusions and report to the class. Asking students open-ended questions and using in-class written exercises also give students an opportunity to participate. Most methods require no special material, no extensive training—simply an understanding of the techniques and a commitment to listen to students (Drueke 1992, 79).

Many of the strategies incorporated into active learning and teaching are familiar to the elementary or secondary teacher or even corporate trainer but not necessarily known to the librarian or university professor.

> Some simple [active learning] ideas for any library instruction setting include information conversations with students before instruction, arrangement of the chairs in a circle or in small groups, allowing thinking time, contributing personal anecdotes to discussions, and asking questions. The most well-known of the techniques described in the literature include: the modified lecture, brainstorming and mindmapping, small group work, cooperative projects, peer teaching and partnering, and writing (Allen 1995, 96).

The use of the strategies, though, must be purposeful. Allen (1995) cautioned that the use of active learning techniques must allow students to see the application of higher order thinking skills or the activities might be considered "busy work—gimmicky and worthless" (99).

To ensure that new approaches to instruction are effective, librarians will need to become curriculum design experts. Resource-based learning is becoming the curriculum change concept of the future. Doyle (1994) noted that

> instead of teacher directed instruction, experience-based learning must become the norm in our schools. Information literacy is not concerned with the restructuring process in itself; however the new experienced-based curricular design is of central importance in information literacy. One textbook expounded by the teacher must be replaced by a program that includes a variety of resources from which students extract needed information—in short, resource-based learning.
>
> Resource-based learning is not the same as resource-based teaching. The latter refers to additional resources the teacher brings into the classroom to broaden instructional practices. The teacher makes all the decisions as to the appropriateness of material. In resource-based learning, the students select the resources they think will best meet their needs for information (34).

The librarian plays the teaching role in helping students to become independent users (access, evaluation, and application) of information.

Knowledge of curriculum design and learning theory allow for use of active learning and teaching strategies in ways that facilitate student learning. Library school programs need to change to reflect the growing emphasis on the educational role of librarians. As librarians design instruction workshops, credit courses, course-integrated sessions, and/or on-line instruction opportunities and incorporate active learning and teaching strategies, knowledge of curriculum design and learning theory will be essential.

> Academic libraries have responded to the computer revolution by incorporating automation processes into their operations. Few question the success libraries have had in these endeavors. But academic libraries obviously need to respond to these other, perhaps more important "revolutions," that specifically identify the students' need for information-seeking skills. Thus curriculum committees in our schools of librarianship need to be concerned and anticipate these changes before we are left behind (McInnis 1995, 16).

The new courses suggested by McInnis (1995) for library schools include Learning Styles and Information Seeking, Ways of Thinking in the Discipline, Research Traditions in Disciplines, and Disciplinary Approaches to Discourse.

Librarians must take a leadership role in instruction especially in the Information Age.

> The increase in complexity of the information environment requires that librarians become proactive in teaching information skills. An expanded library user education program will include teaching the structure of information, use of new electronic formats, and applying critical thinking to information. Librarians will have to maximize the use of technology to teach more skills to greater numbers of users. . . . The emphasis will be on problem solving and on obtaining and accessing information rather than on ownership. User instruction will need to provide students and faculty with basic, intermediate, and advanced guidance in use of the library (Tiefel 1995, 329).

During this time of change, librarians need to examine traditional services for efficiency and effectiveness and to explore new models for delivery of information. The demands for instruction services will continue to explode as greater access to information becomes readily available. Users will be confronted with the need to determine what they need to know, to sort through large databases, to critically assess the relevance of information found, and to effectively use the information in decision-making and problem-solving. Librarians will be teachers.

> Librarians can no longer question their educational purpose— they do have a role to play in teaching users. Librarians must go beyond their present efforts and attempt to form additional teaching partnerships with faculty, allocate additional funds and staff, and develop innovative and dynamic means of communicating the attitudes, awareness, skills and knowledge that all students need (Rader and Coons 1992, 120).

A dichotomy created with the explosion of technology and user access to information is the ability to create systems designed for independent use and the need for instruction is using those systems.

> In the short term, as capacity increases, students will require more instruction and training and more help with transformation and identifying quality information.
> Truly reaching students will take more than a combination of networks, books, digital content, and servers.

Strategic relationships—human connections that mirror the networks that students are using—are also needed. The most effective academic information services for undergrads involve people from the library, campus computing, and the teaching faculty. Cooperation on staff training, triage, and referrals is needed to insure that students receive well-informed advice from staff at the most appropriate level (Alberico 1995, 32).

Shirato and Badics (1997) replicated the LOEX Surveys in 1995. The format and content of questions remained essentially the same with a few questions added about on-line catalogs and other electronic sources. One significant finding was the decreased reliance on workbooks and handbooks for faculty and students. Shorter, current guides to research tools were the most popular print sources and use of these guides increased by 12 percent from the 1987 survey. The other significant area of increased activity, a seven percent increase, was required participation in course-related instruction activities. Six areas of activity on the survey remained stable when compared to the 1987 survey: credit courses, separate administration of instruction programs, lectures, use of bibliographies and pathfinders, use of computer-assisted instruction, and use of videotapes. The remaining nine areas of activity experienced decreases including the virtual disappearance of use of transparencies and slidetapes.

The most effective instruction methods listed were "hands-on; individual instruction; lectures combined with some other methods such as hands-on practice; and active learning methods. The least effective methods most frequently mentioned were lectures; tours of all varieties; print handouts; and workbooks" (Shirato and Badics 1997, 234). When summarizing the results, the authors noted: "It is clear that many methods used in the 70s and 80s are no longer being used. Newer methods, of course are being used . . ." (235). It appears that instruction librarians are designing instruction methods that are compatible with the learning model proposed by Barr and Tagg. The most frequently mentioned effective methods reflect the student-centered orientation of the learning model; the most frequently mentioned, less effective methods are teacher-centered or expert-based modes of the traditional instructional model.

As instruction librarians create new learning experiences and use new methods, traditional methods and modes of providing library instruction will be replaced. Collaboration with faculty, for example, creates the opportunity for more librarians to be in the teaching classroom and to have library use integrated into the curriculum of a course, as well as into the curriculum of the institution. Technology allows the instruction needs of students who are not in the library and/or who want to choose the timing and method of their learning to be met. As instruction becomes more student-centered, librarians can explore the effective practice of students learning from other students. Graduate and undergraduate students serve as mentors, tutors, laboratory assistants, research assistants, and teaching assistants. Using students in instructional roles in the library is an area worth examining. The library is often a site of student-to-student learning. Public service librarians observe student-to-student transfer of knowledge taking place in group study rooms or at computer terminals. Librarians will be challenged to partner with students to provide instruction. This is a major shift in how librarians view the abilities of others, including teaching faculty, to deliver information concerning library use. However, librarians observe the fact that students do teach other students. Librarians can best guide that teaching and learning process by being actively involved in designing and incorporating it into library instruction programs.

Several academic libraries report using students to provide technical assistance, on-line catalog information support, and CD-ROM and other electronic database searching assistance. At the University of New Mexico General Library, students are trained as library-instruction peer tutors and, primarily through one-on-one appointments, provide assistance for searching information databases including the on-line catalog, electronic databases in FirstSearch, and the Web. Peer tutors also assist librarians, who conduct instruction workshops by guiding students through hands-on portions of the workshops as needed. Higher education institutions have long histories of fostering peer learning. Libraries can use this effective model to further the learning opportunities of students.

REFERENCES

Alberico, Ralph. 1995. Serving college students in an era of recombinant information. *Wilson Library Bulletin* 69 (March): 29–32.

Allen, Eileen E. 1995. Active learning and teaching. In *Library instruction revisited: Bibliographic instruction comes of age,* edited by Lynne E. Martin. New York: Haworth Press.

American Library Association Presidential Committee on Information Literacy. 1989. Final Report. Chicago: American Library Association.

Barr, Robert B., and John Tagg. 1995. From teaching to learning—A new paradigm for undergraduate education. *Change* 27 (6): 12–25.

Behrens, Shirley J. 1994. A conceptual analysis and historical overview of information literacy. *College & Research Libraries* 55 (4): 309–322.

Breivik, Patricia Senn. 1985. Information literacy. *American Libraries* 16 (10): 723.

Coughlin, Caroline M., and Alice Gertzog. 1992. *Lyle's administration of the college library.* 5th ed. Metuchen, N.J.: Scarecrow Press.

Demo, William. 1986. The idea of "information literacy" in the age of high-tech. ERIC Document 282 537.

Doyle, Christina S. 1994. Information literacy in an information society: A concept for the information age. Washington, D.C.: Office of Educational Research and Improvement. ERIC Document 372 763.

Drueke, Jeanetta. 1992. Active learning in the university library instruction classroom. *Research Strategies* 10 (2): 77–83.

Farber, Evan Ira. 1995. Bibliographic instruction, briefly. In *Information for a new age: Redefining the librarian,* comp. Library Instruction Round Table, 23–34. Englewood, Colo.: Libraries Unlimited.

Garfield, Eugene. 1979. 2001: An information society? *Journal of Information Science* 1 (2): 210–212.

Guskin, Alan E., Carla J. Stoffle, and Joseph A. Boisse. 1979. The academic library as a teaching library: A role for the 1980s. *Library Trends* 28 (Fall): 281–296.

Holmes-Wong, Deborah, Marianne Afifi, Shahla Behavar, and Xioyang Liu. 1997. If you build it, they will come: Spaces, values, and services in the digital era. *Library Administration and Management* 11 (2): 74–85.

Hopkins, Frances L. 1982. A century of bibliographic instruction: The historical claim to professional and academic legitimacy. *College & Research Libraries* 43 (3): 192–198.

Horton, Forest Woody Jr. 1983. Information literacy vs. computer literacy. *Bulletin of the American Society for Information Science* 9 (4): 14–16.

Kirkendall, Carolyn. 1980. Library use education: Current practices and trends. *Library Trends* 29 (1): 29–37.

Knapp, Patricia. 1966. *The Monteith College library experiment.* New York: Scarecrow Press.

McInnis, Raymond. 1995. Why library schools need to change their curriculum. Washington, D.C.: Office of Educational Research and Improvement. ERIC Document 400 821.

Mensching, Teresa B. 1989. Trends in bibliographic instruction in the 1980s: A comparison of data from two surveys. *Research Strategies* 17 (1): 4–13.

Rader, Hannelore, and William Coons. 1992. Information literacy: One response to the new decade. In *The evolving educational mission of the library*, eds. Betsy Baker and Mary Ellen Litzinger, 109–127. Chicago: Association of College and Research Libraries.

Robinson, Otis Hall. 1880. College libraries as aids to instruction: Rochester University Library—administration and use. In *User instruction in academic libraries*, comps. Hardesty, Larry L., John P. Schmitt, and John Mark Tucker, 17–34. Metuchen, N.J.: Scarecrow Press.

Rubin, Richard. 1977. Azariah Smith Root and library instruction at Oberlin College. *Journal of Library History* 12 (3): 250–261.

Shirato, Linda, and Joseph Badics. 1997. Library instruction in the 1990s: A comparison with trends in two earlier LOEX surveys. *Research Strategies* 15 (4): 223–237.

Taylor, Robert S. 1979. Reminiscing about the future: Professional education and the information environment. *Library Journal* 104 (1): 1871–1875.

Tiefel, Virginia M. 1995. Library user education: Examining its past, projecting its future. *Library Trends* 44 (2): 318–338.

Tompkins, Philip. 1990. New structures for teaching libraries. *Library Administration and Management* 4 (2): 77–81.

Tucker, John Mark. 1984. Emerson's library legacy: Concepts in bibliographic instruction. In *Increasing the teaching role of academic libraries*, ed. Thomas G. Kirk, 15–24. San Francisco: Jossey-Bass.

Wiegand, Wayne. 1996. *A biography of Melvil Dewey: Irrepressible reformer*. Chicago: American Library Association.

Winsor, Justin. 1894. The development of the library: Address at dedication of the Orrington Lunt Library. *Library Journal* 19 (11): 370–375.

Zurkowski, Paul G. 1974. The information service environment relationships and priorities. Washington, D.C.: National Program for Library and Information Services. ERIC Document 100 391.

ADDITIONAL READINGS

Breivik, Patricia Senn, and Robert Wedgeworth, eds. 1988. *Libraries and the search for academic excellence.* Metuchen, N.J.: Scarecrow Press.

Breivik, Patricia Senn, and E. Gordon Gee. 1989. *Information literacy: Revolution in the library.* The American Council on Education/Macmillan Series on Higher Education. New York: Macmillan.

Grimes, Deborah J. 1993. The library-classroom link: History, theory, and application. Paper presented at the 2nd Cooperative Ventures Conference of the Combined Media Organizations of Georgia, 9 March 1990, at Jekyll Island, Georgia. Revised 1993. ERIC Document 364 227.

Keefer, Jane. 1993. The hungry rats syndrome: Library anxiety, information literacy and the academic reference process. In *Library literacy*, ed. Mary Reichel. *RQ* 32 (3): 333–338.

Lipow, Anne Grodzins, ed. 1993. *Rethinking reference in academic libraries*, Proceeding and Process of Library Solutions Institute No. 2 at University of California, Berkeley, March 12–14, 1993 and Duke University, June 4–6, 1993. Berkeley: Library Solutions Press.

MacAdam, Barbara. 1990. Information literacy: Models for the curriculum. *College & Research Libraries News* 51 (10): 948–951.

Pacey, Phillip. 1995. Teaching user education, learning information skills; or, towards the self-explanatory library. *The New Review of Academic Librarianship* (1): 95–103.

Rader, Hannelore. 1990. Bibliographic instruction or information literacy. *College & Research Libraries News* 51 (1): 18, 20.

———. 1995. Information literacy and the undergraduate curriculum. *Library Trends* 44 (2): 270–278.

———. 1996. User education and information literacy for the next decade: An international perspective. *Reference Services Review* 24 (2): 71–75.

Reichel, Mary, and Mary Ann Ramey, ed. 1987. *Conceptual frameworks for bibliographic education: Theory into practice.* Littleton, Colo.: Libraries Unlimited.

Rice-Lively, Mary Lynn, and J. Drew Racine. 1997. The role of academic librarians in the era of information technology. *Journal of Academic Librarianship* 23 (1): 31–41.

Snavely, Loanne, and Natasha Cooper. 1997. The information literacy debate. *Journal of Academic Librarianship* 23 (1): 9–14.

White, Herbert S. 1992. Bibliographic instruction, information literacy, and information empowerment. *Library Journal* 117 (1): 76–77.

Woodruff, Edwin H. 1886. University libraries and seminary methods of instruction. *Library Journal* 11 (8-9): 219–224.

Chapter 2

Peer Tutoring in Higher Education and Academic Libraries

HISTORY OF PEER TEACHING AND TUTORING

Peer teaching may have first become part of formal education during ancient Greek and Roman times. Older students often helped younger students acquire the skills of rhetoric by providing assistance during recitation sessions. Although it has been suggested that Aristotle used peer teaching, Quintilian, a Spaniard who was the head of Rome's leading school of oratory from A.D. 69 to 88, is often credited with suggesting the use of peer teaching. He noted that younger students benefited from the opportunity to learn from older students. Peer teaching was not seen during the Middle Ages when education was limited to the few and was generally not of high quality. During the Renaissance and the Reformation, peer teaching was found in schools in Germany and England and within the educational process practiced by the Jesuits. During the seventeenth and eighteenth centuries, the British Isles and France were the only countries in which peer teaching was reported in regular use. In the nineteenth century, the mutual or monitoring system of schooling was popular in England, much of the European continent, and in the United States.

In the monitoring system, the teacher instructs student monitors to teach the pupils in the school. Seen as an inexpensive method of educating large numbers of students, the system gained wide acceptance as a strategy for teaching the poor. In the mid-1800s, those for whom the system had been created in the United States demanded access to the more formal systems available to the privileged classes. The desire for more universal systems of education supported by public taxes resulted in the demise of the mutual or monitoring system. During the late nineteenth and early twentieth centuries, little mention is made of peer teaching in the United States with the exception of the one-room schoolhouses found throughout rural America. With only limited mention of peer teaching or tutoring until the 1950s, the use of peers in

the educational process has greatly expanded with a resurgence of peer instruction beginning in the 1960s (Wagner 1982).

With the open admissions policies of many institutions of higher education during the 1960s and 1970s, the need for remediation for large numbers
of students resulted in peer-tutoring services. Peer tutoring differed from previous peer teaching endeavors by emphasizing peer assistance as an adjunct
to instruction provided by a teacher in the classroom rather than emphasizing
peer assistance as replacing the teacher. Although institutions varied in their
approaches to handling the needs of scores of underprepared students, many
colleges and universities initiated remedial or developmental courses supported with peer-tutoring services. This period saw the development of centralized learning centers that offered peer tutoring and/or peer counseling.

> During the latter part of this decade [1970s], college assis-
> tance programs began to be offered in one center or coordi-
> nated from a central office. . . .
>
> Two types of learning centers tended to appear on
> college campuses: (1) those spawned from reading labora-
> tories and study skills programs; and (2) those which
> emerged from libraries and audiovisual centers. There ap-
> peared to be little conformity in function or purpose of the
> centers. Most were organized according to institutional
> needs and the philosophy of the center's administrator
> (Dempsey 1985, 34–35).

Today, learning assistance in the form of remedial instruction or tutoring is
available in colleges and universities. The U.S. Department of Education has
reported that "89 percent of four-year colleges offer some form of remedial instruction or tutoring" (Fact sheet on vouchers 1995, 32). This trend is particularly noteworthy because of the pressures during the 1980s and 1990s to raise
academic standards, especially for admissions, but, at the same time, to educate a more diverse student population. Institutional resources became more
limited, but financial aid opportunities for students were expanded. Casazza
and Silverman (1996) predict a continuing role for learning assistance programs and describe current pressures as tension from

> the ongoing attempts to reconcile democratic ideals with a
> traditional educational system. The argument has revolved
> around how to maintain standards while opening the doors
> to an increasingly diverse student body. Educators discov-
> ered that is it not enough simply to open the doors of higher
> education; schools must be willing to provide the academic
> support necessary to maximize the potential of all their
> students.

Because the students enrolling in colleges and universities will continue to represent a broad range of talents and backgrounds, learning assistance and developmental education programs will be an integral part of the educational system for a long time to come (33–34).

Tutoring programs have expanded from initial remedial roles to comprehensive service programs, providing assistance to any student, not just those identified as underprepared. Peer assistance with writing, math, science, and languages, in addition to study skills and reading, are common elements of many learning center tutorial programs. One of the first such comprehensive programs was established in southern California in 1972. The centralized program, designed to serve the university community, included reading, math, and writing centers with professional and peer tutors; opportunities for self-paced programmed instruction; study skills and standardized test preparation assistance; and a conversation center for foreign students (Christ 1984). Casazza and Silverman (1996) noted services provided through learning assistance programs at four institutions of higher education. These services varied in size, type of degree programs supported, funding structure (public or private), and reporting lines (academic or student services). All the programs provided some type of group-based instruction—either coursework or workshops, and three of the four programs offered peer tutoring assistance. One program made Supplemental Instruction available.

Peer teaching or tutoring is evident to varying degrees throughout the history of formal education. With many colleges currently offering tutoring services, the authors recognize peer-tutoring assistance as an accepted form of instruction for college and university students. Exploring the benefits of tutoring results in a strong basis for applying peer assistance to library instruction.

EFFECTS OF PEER TUTORING ON ACADEMIC PERFORMANCE OF COLLEGE STUDENTS

Lidren, Meier, and Brigham (1991) reported on the effects of maximal and minimal peer tutoring on a group of 193 undergraduate students enrolled in two sections of an introductory psychology course. Using an experimental approach, students volunteered to participate in tutorials or in other departmental research projects. Students who did not volunteer for tutorials were considered the control groups for the respective maximal and minimal experimental groups. One group of students was assigned to small group tutorials that met for one hour each week. Students were required to bring two relevant questions to each tutorial session. This tutoring format was termed maximal peer tutoring. The students assigned to the minimal peer-tutoring format met for one hour each week in groups of 20 or 21 students. The students were required to attend sessions but were not required to bring questions to the tutorial sessions. Students who participated in the maximal and minimal peer-tutoring formats achieved at higher levels than their respective control groups. The effect of the maximal approach was greater than the effect of the minimal approach.

House and Wohlt (1990) studied the effect of participation in a tutoring program on the academic performance of underprepared college freshmen. All students in the study were admitted to a large public university through a special admissions process and were of traditional age. All the students enrolled in 12 credit hours per semester, taking four required courses and four electives during the freshman year. Participation in the tutoring program was voluntary. Slightly more than half of the students did not participate in the tutoring program, with 36 percent participating for one semester and 11 percent participating for both semesters. Results indicated that students who participated in tutoring completed more credit hours than those students who did not participate; all students attempted the same number of hours. Also, male students who participated in the tutoring program achieved higher cumulative grade point averages than those who did not participate. No difference was found for female students.

Robert and Thomson (1994) assessed the impact of several aspects of learning assistance offered to underrepresented students at the University of California, Berkeley. The Student Learning Center (SLC) provides adjunct classes; writing workshops; study groups in math, natural and social sciences, and business administration; and peer-tutoring services.

> Participation in Student Learning Center support services has consistently been related to increased levels of classroom achievement. While combined verbal/math SAT scores for lower division SLC users are substantially lower than the average for lower division students (1090 versus 1220), overall grade point averages of users (2.90 on a scale where A = 4) and nonusers (2.95) do not differ significantly (12).

Longuevan and Shoemaker (1991) discovered a positive relationship between participation in tutoring services and expected grade point averages for a group of underprepared students enrolled in six academic courses. Students who did not choose to participate in tutorial sessions achieved higher grades overall due to high entering characteristics such as high school grade point averages in five of the six courses. However, underprepared students who did choose to participate in tutorial sessions made significantly higher grades than was predicted based on standardized test scores and high school grades.

> In every case where it was possible to predict course grades, the obtained average course grade for students in TAP [Tutorial Assistance Program] was larger than the predicted average course grade. That is, the TAP students

actually earned higher grades, on average, than what would expected if they had not attended TAP. We therefore conclude that TAP tutoring was effective for these groups of students in these six courses, Fall 1990 (6).

Topping (1996) reviewed the literature of peer tutoring in further and higher education. Nine formats for peer tutoring were included in the review: cross-year; small group tutoring; the Personalized System of Instruction, or Keller, system; Supplemental Instruction; same-year dyadic fixed-role tutoring; same-year dyadic reciprocal peer tutoring; dyadic cross-year fixed-role peer tutoring; same-year group tutoring; peer-assisted writing; and peer-assisted distance learning. Topping noted that peer tutoring in a variety of formats is widely used in higher education. Characteristics of peer tutoring include a focus on curriculum content; specific procedures for interaction between tutor and tutee in which the tutor, at least, has received training; structured materials in which the tutee has some choice; and specific roles for tutor and tutee. Although there are examples of quantitative research into peer tutoring, Topping found that most research in the area is descriptive in nature and suggested that future research focus on the quality of design and definitions and measures of success. Topping also noted that tutoring is often effective when measured in terms of program goals and suggested that broader measures be employed.

Maxwell (1990) encouraged professionals in the field of developmental education to assess the effectiveness of peer tutoring on the achievement of underprepared students. Maxwell also noted that much research is focused on subjective outcomes and tutee evaluations of tutors and/or services. Research does not consistently show that tutoring makes a difference in terms of academic success for underprepared students. However, underprepared students who participate in tutoring services are retained longer than similar students who do not participate. Students who do earn better grades after participating in tutoring services are generally higher in ability than underprepared students. Maxwell encouraged further study of the effectiveness of tutoring, incorporating objective as well as subjective measures.

TUTOR TRAINING: ESSENTIAL ELEMENT FOR PROGRAM SUCCESS

In effective tutoring programs, tutor training is seen as essential for program success (Robert and Thomson 1994; House and Wohlt 1990; Longuevan and Shoemaker 1991; Lidren et al. 1991). Medway (1991) reviewed studies that focused on the social psychology of tutoring and concluded that "peer instructors will not naturally employ good teaching strategies and appropriate use of reinforcement unless trained and monitored" (22). Rings and Sheets (1991) proposed eight fundamental topics for tutor training based on student-development philosophy and metacognitive theory: self-directed learning (student development); effective communication skills; referrals to campus resources; availability of support materials; learning theory and learning styles; metacognition; cultural diversity; and strategies for assisting students with learning disabilities. Hartman (1990) proposed that the goal of tutoring is more than simply to impart skills or knowledge; in addition, the goal of tutoring is to create self-directed or independent learners. Tutors should be trained to teach tutees using methods that empower them to eventually direct their own learning. This can be accomplished by recognizing the complexity of factors that affect the tutoring interaction and incorporating those factors into training and program development. The identified factors are cognitive variables, metacognition and cognition, affective variables, and the environmental context (academic and nonacademic).

Council for Advancement of Standards for Student Services/Development Programs Guidelines

In 1986, after six years of work involving a number of professional associations, the Council for the Advancement of Standards (CAS) for Student Services/Development Programs published and disseminated "Standards and Guidelines for Student Services/Development Programs." These guidelines outlined general standards for a variety of student-services-oriented programs, along with functional standards for sixteen areas including learning assistance. The guidelines are "beneficial in identifying staff development activities, conducting self-studies, evaluating programs and services, setting goals and establishing priorities" (Materniak and Williams 1987, 12). Functional goals for learning assistance include the adequate training and supervision of paraprofessional staff including undergraduate or graduate students.

College Reading and Learning Association International Tutor Training Certification Program

In 1989, the College Reading and Learning Association (CRLA) established a tutor training certification program. Through documented adherence to tutor hiring, training, and evaluation criteria, tutoring programs could receive certification. Certification allows programs to certify tutors at three levels of expertise—Regular, Advanced, and Master. Programs can seek certification at one, two, or all three levels. Initial certification is for a one-year period with recertification required at the end of the year. The second certification is for a three-year period, and the third certification is for a five-year period. All subsequent certifications are in effect for five years. (See Appendix A for a list of the more than 400 certified programs).

Tutor hiring criteria include grades of A or B in the courses to be tutored or direct evidence of equivalent experience. In addition, an interview with the tutor trainer or supervisor and either a recommendation from relevant instructors or from the tutor trainer or supervisor is required. The interview is an especially important part of the process; during the interview, the potential tutor can demonstrate interpersonal characteristics relevant to establishing effective tutoring relationships (CRLA 1998).

Specific training topics are required at each level of certification, and a variety of training methods must be used. For example, topics required for the Regular Certificate include tutor responsibilities, basic tutoring do's and don'ts, and active listening and paraphrasing. Topics at the Advanced Level include learning styles, cultural diversity, use of probing queries, and subject area training. Master Level topics include assertiveness training, group dynamics, and supervisory skills. The Advanced and Master Levels include a review of previous training topics. At each level, the programs may include other topics related to specific needs of the program. Tutors must participate in a minimum of 10 hours of training to receive each certificate. A tutor who receives a Master Certificate would have completed a minimum of 30 hours of training (CRLA 1998).

To receive certification, a tutor evaluation program must be documented. The evaluation process must occur regularly, and tutors must receive the feedback from the process. It is not sufficient to conduct only program evaluations; the work of individual tutors must be assessed. A minimum of 25 hours of tutoring experience is needed at each level of certification. A tutor who receives a Master Level certificate would have accrued a minimum of 75 hours of actual tutoring experience. Although not delineated in the certification guidelines, tutors are expected to receive satisfactory evaluations on a regular basis and to correct any deficiencies noted before achieving the next level of certification (CRLA 1998; see Appendix A for detailed criteria of each certification level and related information).

LIBRARY PEER ASSISTANCE PROGRAMS

With the widespread existence of peer-tutoring programs in higher education, the historical relationship between learning centers and libraries, and the current trends in library instruction described in Chapter 1, it would be expected that some libraries have engaged in peer-tutoring services. Evidence of peer learning is widely available in libraries; study group rooms are often in use, and classmates often work together on class projects. Some libraries have formalized peer learning experiences by establishing peer assistance programs in a variety of forms.

Peer Information Counseling at the
University of Michigan Undergraduate Library

The Peer Information Counseling (PIC) Program was established at the University of Michigan Undergraduate Library in 1985 to improve the retention of undergraduate minority students. Three assumptions were used in designing the program: first, that library research and information management skills are essential for academic success and, second, that minority students in particular may find using a large research library an intimidating process. The third assumption was "that one of the best resources for helping minority students succeed is the influence of successful minority students themselves" (MacAdam and Nichols 1989, 205). Peer information counselors assisted students in the reference area of the library by helping with activities such as selection of the proper library index, catalog, or database; determining appropriate subject headings; conducting reference interviews; and recognizing the need to make a referral to a librarian. Counselors also provided assistance with writing term papers, especially in the areas of research and of using word processing software. Writing instructional materials and publicizing the PIC program were the other main duties of the counselors. Librarians, student program users, and peer counselors rated the program as effective. Librarians were impressed with the performance of the counselors especially in the area of positive public service attitude. Students who used the services found it very valuable and encouraged its continuation and growth. Counselors enjoyed the opportunity to help others and also noted the benefit of greater expertise in computer use and library research for their own studies.

The Peer Advisory Library Instruction Program at Binghamton University

Stelling (1996) reported the use of peer library assistance at Binghamton University. Undergraduate students enrolled in a course in the School of Education and Human Development were required to research a contemporary social issue using library periodical resources. Although librarians had traditionally conducted one-hour instruction sessions for the students in the course, it was apparent that the sessions were not successful in meeting the needs of all students. As evidenced by inquiries at the reference desk, students with limited computer skills and those students who were novice library-system users needed more assistance. In 1993, a librarian and the school's academic advisor decided to train a group of peer advisors to be library instruction peer advisors as well. The Peer Advisor Library Instruction Program was first introduced during the fall 1993 semester. At that time, only one peer advisor was trained to provide library instruction assistance; the advisor attended instruction sessions conducted by librarians, offered to tutor students individually, and encouraged hands-on practice. Only two students used tutoring services that semester. The program, though, was expanded during subsequent semesters with as many as seven advisors trained as library instruction advisors. Training consisted of learning to conduct searches using Binghamton library resources and the Internet and to assess the appropriateness of library sources. Peer advisors were required to complete an annotated bibliography of sources on a topic of their choice, with requirements tied to specific sources and types of information.

Providing library instruction through the use of the existing Peer Advisory Program was an effective means of reaching more students in need by offering instruction in a supportive, non-threatening environment . . . As the number of nontraditional students continues to increase and the library's electronic tools continue to evolve, the Peer Advisory Library Instruction Program will continue to supplement the classroom instructional session with personalized library instruction (Stelling 1996, 54).

Information Literacy Peer Tutoring Program at Mercy College

In 1993, Mercy College developed plans for three major information literacy initiatives. The first two initiatives were directed at increasing the number of course-integrated instruction activities and at developing an information literacy outcome assessment plan. The third initiative was to develop an information literacy peer tutoring program (Klavano and Kulleseid 1995). The job description designed for the peer tutors included the primary duties of assisting students and faculty in locating and using materials in the library and accessing sources of materials not owned by the library; training students and faculty to use a variety of equipment in the library; finding answers to factual reference questions and making referrals to reference librarians when warranted; helping students to select appropriate search strategies and sources; assisting students and faculty in the use of on-line sources; developing brief bibliographies and guides; and assisting librarians with preparation of instruction sessions. The training materials were aimed at orienting tutors to job duties and expectations and at helping them to develop expertise in automated library systems. Supervisors discussed worksheets and suggested readings with tutors. Librarians and tutors evaluated the program as positive with some reservations.

The actual duties performed by tutors varied widely from location to location. Some performed routine library tasks associated more closely with other student jobs such as shelving materials, filing cards, and servicing copy machines. Most peer tutors did provide assistance to patrons using on-line workstations. Most librarians who worked with tutors reported that the assistance with using computer terminals and in searching databases was the most important role of the tutors. Reservations included assessment and training issues:

> Librarians are particularly concerned with evaluation of the peer tutor's performance and impact on students' overall acquisition of information literacy skills. Since the underprepared Mercy student has special trouble in formulating a good question, can a peer tutor be trained to recognize and refer or sharpen unfocused or misleading questions—such as "Help me get something about dreams"—when the

amount of training time is limited? (Klavano and Kulleseid 1995, 375).

The Reference Assistant Project at the University of Wisconsin–Parkside

The Reference Assistant Project (RAP) at the University of Wisconsin–Parkside was started in 1980 with funding from the Minority Programs Office. Upper-division minority students were trained to provide assistance to students, primarily freshmen, enrolled in two introductory English courses in which specific library assignments must be completed. "The rationale for the project was to provide student-to-student interaction in order to encourage minority students to use library facilities and therefore not delay completing their library competency requirements during the normal time period" (Dawkins and Jackson 1986, 4). The Reference Assistants primarily answered directional, factual, or research strategy questions. The Reference Assistants helped students use reference tools directly related to specific course assignments, which included the completion of a library skills workbook. Evaluations of the service indicated that students found the service to be valuable, noting that the Reference Assistants were easy to approach and very helpful in guiding students through the use of reference sources.

Training and Service Issues of Library Peer Assistance Programs

When we compare the training programs of these library peer assistance programs to CAS and CRLA criteria, it becomes apparent that libraries can benefit from professional standards and guidelines from the field of learning assistance. Library personnel tend to emphasize the acquisition of library information and skills in library-based training. Using guidelines from the field of learning assistance, library trainers would incorporate, for example, learning theory and cognition skills, interpersonal communication skills, and strategies for working with students with learning disabilities into library tutor-training programs. Because peer assistance is not a traditional component of library instruction services, library personnel often lack experience with and knowledge of peer learning principles and programs. Dawkins and Jackson (1986) specifically noted that

> since student reference assistants must be properly trained, more formal training sessions are being developed. . . . One of the main objectives of such a training manual is to have a document that will provide consistent training for student participants in the program as well as to allow students do some of the training on their own through programmed exercises to acquaint them with the services and facilities of the library (6).

In addition to training issues, the infrastructure for providing tutoring services may not readily exist in many libraries. Although library tutors could work at information desks or provide assistance at library workstations, there are often no accommodations for private, one-on-one tutoring sessions. Library tutors might conduct small group instruction sessions but would often compete with other library personnel for limited, well-equipped instruction space.

If peer assistance is to become recognized as a legitimate form of library instruction, the foundations of peer-tutoring programs must be understood. In the following chapter, we introduce the elements of peer-tutoring programs, from philosophy to program evaluation. These elements provide the framework for successful peer-tutoring ventures and can aid librarians in making decisions about essential tutoring program attributes.

REFERENCES

Casazza, Martha E., and Sharon L. Silverman. 1996. *Learning assistance and developmental education: A guide for effective practice.* San Francisco: Jossey-Bass.

Christ, Frank. 1984. Learning assistance at California State University—Long Beach, 1972–1984. *Journal of Developmental & Remedial Education* 8 (2): 2–5.

College Reading and Learning Association. 1998. *The international tutor training certification program.* Rev. ed. Duplicated. (See Appendix A).

Dawkins, Willie Mae, and Jeffrey Jackson. 1986. Enhancing reference services: Students as assistants. *Technicalities* 6 (8): 4–7.

Dempsey, Beverly June Luke. 1985. An update on the organization and administration of learning assistance programs in U.S. senior institutions of higher education. ERIC Document 257 334.

Fact sheet on vouchers: Argument and evidence. 1995. *American Educator* 19 (3): 28, 31–33.

Hartman. Hope J. 1990. Factors affecting the tutoring process. *Journal of Developmental Education* 14 (2): 2–4, 6.

House, J. Daniel, and Victoria Wohlt. 1990. The effect of tutoring program participation on the performance of academically underprepared college freshmen. *Journal of Student Development* 31 (4): 365–370.

Klavano, Ann M., and Eleanor R. Kulleseid. 1995. Bibliographic instruction: Renewal and transformation in one academic library. In *Library instruction revisited: Bibliographic Instruction comes of age,* edited by Lynne M. Martin. New York: Haworth Press.

Lidren, Donna M., Steven E. Meier, and Thomas A. Brigham. 1991. The effects of minimal and maximal peer tutoring systems on the academic performance of college students. *The Psychological Record* 41 (1): 69–77.

Longuevan, Craig, and Judith Shoemaker. 1991. Using multiple regression to evaluate a peer-tutoring program for undergraduates. Paper presented at annual meeting of the California Educational Research Association, 14–15 November 1991, at San Diego, California. ERIC Document 341 717.

MacAdam, Barbara, and Darlene P. Nichols. 1989. Peer information counseling: An academic library program for minority students. *The Journal of Academic Librarianship* 15 (September): 204–209.

Materniak, Georgine, and Audrey Williams. 1987. "CAS standards and guidelines for learning assistance programs." *Journal of Developmental Education* 11 (1): 11–18.

Maxwell, Martha. 1990. Does tutoring help? A look at the literature. *Review of Research in Developmental Education* vol. 7 (4).

Medway, Frederic J. 1991. A social psychological analysis of peer tutoring. *Journal of Developmental Education* 15 (1): 20–26, 32.

Rings, Sally, and Rick A. Sheets. 1991. Student development and metacognition: Foundations for tutor training. *Journal of Developmental Education* 15 (1): 30–32.

Robert, Ellen R., and Gregg Thomson. 1994. Learning assistance and the success of underrepresented students at Berkeley. *Journal of Developmental Education* 17 (3): 4–14.

Stelling, Prue. 1996. Student to student: Training peer advisors to provide BI. *Research Strategies* 14 (Winter): 50–55.

Topping, K. 1996. The effectiveness of peer tutoring in further and higher education: A typology and review of the literature. *Higher Education* 32 (3): 321–345.

Wagner, Lilya. 1982. *Peer teaching historical perspectives*. Westport, Conn.: Greenwood Press.

ADDITIONAL READING

Downing, Karen E., Barbara MacAdam, and Darlene P. Nichols. 1993. *Reaching a multicultural student community: A handbook for academic librarians*. Westport, Conn.: Greenwood Press.

Chapter 3

Foundations of a Peer Tutoring Program

Regardless of specific program services, peer tutoring programs share some fundamental characteristics. An understanding of these characteristics will help librarians create an appropriate context for a library instruction tutoring program and to avoid mistakes that could have a negative impact on the success of the program. These features include program philosophy; expectations of tutors; tutor recruitment, hiring, training, and evaluation; program services; and program evaluation.

PROGRAM PHILOSOPHY

As with any organization, a stated philosophy provides the context for program services (including policies and procedures), and for program infrastructure.

> A myth seems to exist among practitioners of many service-oriented fields that philosophy is the exclusive domain of a few select academicians. However, the application (of philosophical thought) to real-life situations depends on how willing practitioners are to reflect on why they do what they do (White and Brockett 1987, 11).

The philosophy of a peer tutoring program is the basis for answers to overarching questions such as what are the goals of the program and what services are offered. It also creates the context for many implementation issues such as the expectations of tutors, the content of the training program, the methods and systems of tutor and program evaluation, and the guidelines for tutee responsibilities.

In higher education peer tutoring settings, a philosophy that addresses students as adult learners is essential. Adult students have the ability and opportunity to form their education in ways that children do not; this ability and the responsibilities of adult learners must be recognized at the post-secondary level. A peer tutoring philosophy should also include beliefs about the role of the teacher (tutor) and the learner (tutee). Beliefs about the value of the learning process are important to the peer tutoring program. Any philosophy used as the foundation for learning assistance through peer tutoring

> is based on a belief system that focuses on maximizing the potential of all learners so that they may meet their goals. The philosophy assumes that to maximize learner potential, responsibility and commitment must be shared by learner and the practitioner. It also assumes that the learning process takes place in a meaningful context and is sensitive to the cognitive, emotional, and social needs of the learner (Casazza and Silverman 1996, 261).

A philosophy will answer questions about the primary role of the tutor: is it to guide, lead, facilitate, and/or help learners identify and solve problems? What is believed about evaluation of outcomes? Is evaluation best done by the tutee, by the tutor, or both? Should evaluation be built into the system or is it not very important because success may come later or be demonstrated in the classroom rather than the tutoring situation? Are differences among tutees important or unimportant? If important, do differences result from cultural and social experiences? Are individual differences minimized as common needs and problems are recognized? What should tutoring methods focus on: problem-solving, practice and feedback, critical thinking, and/or learner responsibility and independence? Do the tutee's feelings provide energy for the learning process or get in the way of the learning process? What is most important when sessions are planned: an end result, clarification of concepts and principles, application of a problem-solving process, or learner needs and desires? Do people learn best through repetition, by interacting with others, from an expert, or when they guide the process? Is most of what people know acquired through an educational process, through self-discovery, through trial and error, through a critical thinking process, or as a result of setting goals (Zinn 1990)?

Paul Bergevin's *A Philosophy for Adult Education*, written in 1967, continues to offer a strong foundation for a variety of adult-focused programs including peer tutoring programs in higher education settings.

> The general concepts and underlying principles used here were first theoretically projected and then had their applicability tested. They have been derived, over a period of 20 years, partly from theory and partly from practice. They are now set forth because they can be translated into useful operational techniques. Experience has shown that they can be adapted to particular programs of adult learning (Bergevin 1967, 4).

Several specific elements of Bergevin's philosophy are that all learners can learn; that learners are responsible for their own learning; that learners are active participants, not passive receivers; that how learners are taught is as important as what they are taught; and that the process is as important as the product. "The adult learning process must become a creating, releasing experience rather than a dulling series of passively attended indoctrination exercises" (Bergevin 1967, 5).

The philosophy's focus on the learning process underscores the principle of lifelong learning, a central theme of modern-day library instruction programs. With the rapid change in information access technology, specific technical information often becomes obsolete before students leave the university. More emphasis is placed on the concepts underlying the search process, the record structure, and the evaluation of information. A philosophy that includes the belief that the process is as important as the product is essential for a library instruction tutoring program.

Embedded in a learning and teaching philosophy are the elements of learning theory. Practitioners need to articulate beliefs about the learning process so that the learning process is supported by and reflected in program services. The works of David Kolb, Jerome Bruner, and David Ausubel, among others, form the basis of current learning theories. Not only do tutors need to understand the adult learning process and how their work can facilitate that process, program services should also reflect beliefs about learning. Tutor training is an obvious opportunity to demonstrate and apply learning theories; tutors should be trained in ways that model the learning theory underlying tutoring strategies. Perhaps less obvious in relationship to learning theory, but just as important, are decisions about program structure. For example, the answers to questions about the frequency and length of tutoring sessions are found in adult learning theory.

A program philosophy can and should be applied to essential program elements—duties and responsibilities of tutors, recruitment and hiring of tutors, tutor training, and tutor evaluations. In the first part of this chapter, we examine specific applications of these program elements. In the latter part of the chapter, we look at applications of adult learning philosophy in terms of program services and evaluations.

EXPECTATIONS OF TUTORS

The role of the tutor as an information provider is a core element of a peer tutoring program. An operating assumption is that the tutor possesses more knowledge of a particular subject or topic than the tutee. If the tutor is functioning solely as an information provider, the tutee comes to the tutor with a question and the tutor provides the answer. This is often the easiest role for both the tutor and tutee. It is often easier for the tutor to provide the answer rather than to explain or demonstrate a problem-solving process.

However, a program based on a philosophy of adult learning principles would conclude that simply supplying the answers is not an appropriate role for the tutor. If the philosophy of the program includes such goals as developing student understanding and fostering learner independence, having the tutor give the answers conflicts with the program philosophy. Instead, the tutor must help the tutee to discover and/or apply a method for finding the answer. Otherwise, the tutee will be dependent on the tutor when confronted with a new problem. The tutor becomes a guide or mentor and models approaches to problem-solving that allow the tutee to discover the answer or to understand a method of finding the answer. This is not to say that a tutor would never provide an answer to a question or problem, but the tutor would do so only within the context of a larger strategy.

An underlying assumption of peer tutoring is that the tutor has taken the same course as the tutee. The tutor and tutee may have had the same professor and very often have used the same textbook. This common experience forms a bond from which a guiding or mentoring relationship is developed. Although the tutor may not have had the same questions as the tutee, the tutor recalls the experience of learning the information and is able to share with the tutee examples, illustrations, and learning strategies that helped the tutor learn the information.

Tutors are expected to work with all students who seek assistance, and to create effective interpersonal relationships with tutees. Tutors must be aware of their own biases and assumptions about issues that affect the tutoring relationship. Most tutors have been very successful as students; how do they, for example, view students who are seeking tutorial assistance? Depending on campus demographics, tutors may work with tutees from a variety of racial and ethnic backgrounds. Tutors must be sensitive to differences among students such as cultural approaches to asking for help, individual communication styles, and learning styles. Tutors must also be sensitive to the needs of students with learning disabilities.

Tutors are expected to be professional in handling confidential information, dealing with difficult tutees, and making decisions about violations of student conduct guidelines. Privacy laws protect much of the information about students. Revealing the identity of a tutee to persons outside of the program could be a violation of privacy. Tutors may have access to Social Security numbers, learning disability diagnoses, and other personal information about tutees. All this information is protected by law. Tutors will also discover what the tutee likes and dislikes about specific courses and professors, information that should not be shared. Knowing how to handle confidential information is an important responsibility of tutors.

Tutors will encounter difficult tutees. Sometimes the difficulty lies in differences in communication styles or differing expectations of the tutoring relationship. Difficult tutees may also demand more than is provided by program guidelines, react to stressful personal and academic challenges in inappropriate ways, or display evidence of mental health problems. Tutors are expected to possess and use strategies that help to salvage difficult situations.

Tutors may also become aware of violations of student codes of conduct such as cheating on examinations or plagiarism of published materials. Sometimes the tutee's mistake is inadvertent but sometimes it is intentional. Because of their academic mastery, tutors may be asked to write a paper or take an examination for a tutee. Under the ruse of helping with ungraded homework assignments, tutors might be asked to complete assignments such as take-home examinations, which are actually turned in for grades. A thorough knowledge of the institution's rules and the program's guidelines is essential for tutors.

Tutors are also expected to be good employees and to represent the program. Tutoring programs will have numerous policies and procedures that affect the tutor's work. Adhering to those policies and procedures will result in an effective work environment for the tutor and program staff. Tutors are also often thrust into the role of program spokesperson, referring friends and classmates to program services and/or describing program services to faculty, friends, and classmates.

RECRUITING AND HIRING TUTORS

Peer tutors are recruited from those students who have been successful in courses or areas for which tutoring is provided. Specific guidelines such as course grades, specific course components of academic majors and minors, and undergraduate or graduate status are also considered when a recruitment plan is developed. Department or college honor rolls, student organizations, and scholarship recipients are just a few of the sources for recruiting tutors. Another area to consider is compensation: Are tutors to be paid, to serve as volunteers, or to receive course credit. Expectations about some program characteristics such as hours worked may vary depending on how the tutor is to be compensated.

The hiring process should include an interview and a standard application packet containing required documents such as transcripts and letters of recommendation. The interview is central to the hiring process. An important part of the tutor's role is to establish an effective interpersonal relationship with the tutee, and much can be learned about the applicant's ability to create such a relationship during the interview. In addition to typical interview questions about work history, strengths, and weaknesses, potential tutors can be asked questions that reveal their understanding of how they learn. Questions that allow them to demonstrate their strategies for academic success may expose personal biases or assumptions. Questions concerning specific content area knowledge are usually not the focus of the interview process. Some programs require applicants to take tests on specific content area knowledge, but many rely on course grades and faculty recommendations as evidence of subject area competency. Appendix B contains some sample interview questions.

Faculty referrals not only provide valuable information on the applicant's academic performance, but also form an important connection between the faculty member and the program. Making recommendations allows the faculty member to be involved in the program and to assume some responsibility for the quality of tutors hired. The contact with faculty also creates an environment in which faculty members will actively refer students to the program. Faculty members will become familiar with program guidelines and expectations. Faculty may be more likely to refer students to tutoring services if the faculty members have been involved in the tutor hiring process.

TRAINING TUTORS

Tutor training programs should be rigorous demonstrations of program philosophy and inherent learning theory. Training programs allow program staff members to model what they extol on tutors as good practice. Tutor training is often the first opportunity for new tutors to meet all program staff and other tutors, to understand the organization of the program, and to grasp how their work fits into the larger program context. Tutor training should be designed to make an important and long-lasting impression on tutors. Training programs generally include three main elements: program orientation, development of tutoring skills, and reinforcement of subject area skills.

Program Orientation

Program orientation should cover all the policies and procedures that have an impact on the work of the tutor. Orientation can be organized from general to specific, from broad to narrow. An effective starting point is the organization of the program including the tutor's supervisor and work team, if applicable, and the relationship among program components. An overview of program services, even those in which the tutor may not be actively involved, is essential to enable the tutor to make good referrals within the program and to be an effective spokesperson for the program. These elements of an orientation program provide the context within which the program exists, as well as the framework for the tutor's role within the program.

Orientations also encompass the more detailed information that the tutor will need to work within the program. Each program has procedures and guidelines that define the workflow of the tutor meeting with the tutee. These might include how appointments are made, how drop-in laboratories are staffed, what happens if a tutee does not attend a scheduled session, and how long the appointment lasts. In addition, each program has paperwork that must be completed. Documentation procedures for contacts with tutees not only contribute to program recordkeeping practices but also provide documentation for payroll purposes. If tutors are to be paid for training and preparation time, in addition to actual tutoring time, the proper documentation for all paid activities is reviewed during orientation.

The expectations of employees (those procedures and guidelines associated with employment in general) are also covered in a tutor orientation program. Specific elements could be topics such as the processes for changing one's work schedule, asking for time off from work, and calling in sick; the availability and location of work space; dress codes; rules for use of work time including studying or eating at work; available materials and equipment; opportunities for advancement; and how performance is evaluated.

Tutoring Skills

Although orientations to the program are necessary and important, they are not sufficient to provide the skills tutors need for successful work with tutees. A tutor training program must also offer the opportunity for tutors to develop tutoring skills and to make connections between learning theory and practice.

Tutoring skills encompass the ability to communicate subject area knowledge in such a manner that the tutee may develop independent learning skills. Tutees develop the ability to think critically about the subject being studied, to understand the context for the information, and to extend the practice of the information into analysis, synthesis, and evaluation. Communication skills are needed to create a professional interpersonal relationship with the tutee. This relationship is one in which the responsibilities of tutor and tutee are clear and in which learning is fostered.

Because many students have not participated in the peer tutoring relationship prior to college, the clarification of the role of tutors is important. Tutees may easily conceive of the tutor as a teacher, someone who is only an expert information provider. The tutee with that expectation will be disappointed when the tutor functions as a guide or mentor, emphasizing tutee learning rather than tutor expertise. Training tutors to make expectations clear, especially in initial tutoring sessions, lays the foundation for a successful relationship. Training often involves a standard introduction that describes what the tutee can expect from tutoring sessions. Through this aspect of training, tutors become skilled at setting the foundation for a tutee-centered working relationship. When the roles of the tutor and tutee are clear, tutee learning is the focus of the tutoring sessions. If the roles are unclear, the relationship between the tutor and tutee too often becomes the focus of the tutoring sessions.

Communication skills are also used to foster tutee learning. Tutors learn to ask questions that will result in tutee reflection, assessment, and self-correction. Tutors learn to wait for tutee responses, to become comfortable with silence, and to restate tutee questions and comments as a process of clarification and concentration. Effective questioning skills keep the focus of the tutoring session on the tutee's needs rather than on the tutor's expertise. These skills also assist the tutor in assessing tutee learning. Effective communication skills allow the tutor to become proficient at starting a tutoring relationship with the proper foundation, focusing on tutee needs during the tutoring session, and concluding a session with the tutee's review of what has been accomplished. With a focus on clarifying and responding to tutee needs, the tutor–tutee interaction is not unlike the reference interview process between the librarian and library patron.

Tutor training programs should also provide opportunities for tutors to make connections between program philosophy and subsequent tutoring practices. The training program allows program philosophy to be presented and tutors to experience that philosophy in action. Observations of mock tutoring and role playing give tutors the chance to safely practice behaviors that support program philosophy. During training sessions, tutors can practice working with tutees who, for example, expect the tutor to do all the work, who accuse the professor of poor teaching, who lack self confidence, and/or who do not readily demonstrate higher order reasoning skills. Not only do these situations require good communication skills, but they also require application of the philosophy of the program. During training sessions, tutors enhance their understanding of the program's philosophy by making decisions based on that philosophy and communicating those decisions in a safe environment.

Subject Area Skills

Reinforcement of subject area skills is an essential element of tutor training. Tutors are hired with an assumption that they possess a certain level of subject area knowledge, as evidenced through course grades and faculty referrals. As students, tutors have demonstrated an acquisition of knowledge. As tutors, though, they must possess an understanding of that information in ways that might not have been assessed during coursework. For example, as students, they may never have been in the position of explaining the information to others. Although they may be competent at solving a problem, writing an essay, or doing research, they may lack an understanding of the concepts that will help others to gain the same knowledge.

As noted in Chapter 2, one way that tutors benefit from the tutoring process is by becoming more expert in the subject area. Incorporating subject area skills into the training process recognizes this element of tutoring. An emphasis on subject area skills also acknowledges that no one tutor can have a complete academic experience. Tutors cannot possess, for example, the experience of taking the same course from several different professors. The textbooks used in a course may have changed since the tutor took the course. Academic departments may change their approach to the teaching of a subject; for example, writing programs may start using portfolios for student assessment in introductory writing courses. Tutors must become acquainted with different textbooks and need to learn how to support new teaching approaches.

Tutor training, which should include trainers with expertise in the training areas, is the responsibility of program staff. In addition to faculty and non-program staff, these trainers should include experienced tutors. Involving faculty members in the training process gives tutors the opportunity to learn from experts and offers the faculty the opportunity to learn more about the tutoring program. Involving faculty members who have introduced new approaches to the subject or who may expect students to use a particular software program, for example, provides needed expertise for tutors. Non-program staff members who possess expertise in customer service are accustomed to making referrals to other campus agencies, or well-versed in cultural differences, for example, can be valuable contributors to a training program.

Again, tutors learn about other resources and non-program staff members learn more about the tutoring program. Using tutors as trainers emphasizes the basic tenet of peer tutoring: the value of learning from others who have similar experiences and needs. Tutor program staff, though, should be the primary trainers, especially of new tutors. Program staff can model program philosophy and good practice in ways that faculty and non-program staff cannot be expected to demonstrate. Using experienced tutors as trainers provides credibility to the basic principles of peer tutoring.

Training Structure

In addition to the initial training of new tutors, an on-going training program must be established to continue developing tutoring skills and subject area expertise. Training for new tutors is most extensive immediately before they begin to tutor. For most post-secondary institutions, new-tutor training is scheduled within one week of the beginning of an academic term. Experienced tutors participate in new-tutor training as trainers and in training sessions specifically designed for returning tutors. Experienced tutors need an overview of changes in policies, procedures, and services in addition to advanced training in communication skills. Training topics such as recognizing learning styles, working with students with learning disabilities, and conducting group-tutoring sessions usually are introduced within training programs for experienced tutors. These advanced topics are more meaningful and relevant to tutors who have mastered the basic responsibilities of tutoring. On-going training during the academic term, which is usually provided by faculty and experienced tutors, generally focuses on enhancing subject area skills.

All elements of training—orientation, skills development, and subject area expertise reinforcement—should be supported with documentation. Employee handbooks that include a statement of philosophy, employee guidelines, program policies and procedures, and subject area practice, are a common form of training support that represent a resource for tutors. As tutors progress through the on-going training process, such handbooks can be expanded. Because it may contain information about expectations and procedures, the handbook can also be considered part of the contract between the tutor and the tutoring program.

Attendance at tutor training sessions, especially sessions for new tutors, should be mandatory. Tutor training dates can be established in advance so that new tutors learn of the dates during the hiring process and can make arrangements to attend. Programs try to hire tutors prior to the scheduled mandatory training sessions. Often, though, circumstances may necessitate hiring tutors after the scheduled mandatory training. Make-up training sessions, which are usually abbreviated sessions that focus on procedures, expectations, and tutoring strategies, should be scheduled for those tutors.

The hiring coordinator decides whether a new tutor hired after the regular new-tutor training program can begin tutoring before attending make-up training. If a new tutor has prior tutoring experience and/or related experience, the tutor may begin working with tutees before the make-up session. However, if the new tutor has no related experience, the tutor may be required to attend the make-up session before beginning to tutor.

EVALUATING TUTORS

Tutors should be evaluated on how well they perform their duties and carry out their responsibilities. Those duties and responsibilities are based on clearly identified program expectations, which are tied to program philosophy. Duties and responsibilities should be described as specific behaviors. The fulfillment of expectations is measured through assessment of those behaviors. Because it is unfair to evaluate employees based on unclear expectations, tutor training sessions and supporting employee manuals should include clear statements of expectations.

Tutors should be evaluated by tutees and by program staff, which may or may not include other tutors. Tutees can best evaluate the nature of the tutoring relationship and the interaction between the tutor and tutee during tutoring sessions. Tutees can assess relationship features including comfort levels, respect, acceptance, and focus on tutee learning needs. Tutees can also assess the tutor's use of strategies such as questioning, reflection, modeling, feedback, and assessment of tutee learning. In some cases, it might be appropriate for tutees to assess the tutor's organizational skills—for example, how well the tutor uses time during tutoring sessions and whether or not they stay on task. Tutees should not be asked to assess behaviors that they do not directly observe. Tutees cannot evaluate, for example, how well a tutor works with other tutors unless cooperation with other tutors is a specific behavior related to the tutee's experience.

Program staff should also evaluate tutors. They can evaluate the duties and responsibilities tied to program operations such as following procedures, reliable attendance and punctuality, and participation in on-going training sessions. Program staff may also receive formal and informal input on tutor performance from tutees. Other tutees and/or other student employees may also be appropriate reviewers of tutor performance. Again, the reviewer should assess those areas of performance that are known to the reviewer. For example, a graduate student supervisor of writing tutors could assess tutor participation in on-going training sessions conducted by the graduate student, but might not be able to assess punctuality unless the graduate student worked at the same time as the tutor. Student employees responsible for scheduling appointments or responsible for processing tutor-generated paperwork could have input on behaviors they observe such as arriving for appointments and submitting paperwork on time.

Program staff can also help tutors evaluate their work by observing tutoring sessions. Staff members, including graduate students or other student supervisors of tutors, can sit in during sessions and/or videotape or audiotape tutoring sessions. Tutors and supervisors are often the best reviewers of specific tutor behaviors. Although tutee evaluations are essential in providing feedback to tutors, tutees are often unaware of the specific strategies that tutors employ and may find it difficult to furnish the detailed information some tutors desire. Direct observation can be intimidating, yet very valuable. Experienced tutors are most likely to seek this level of assessment. Some form of direct observation can be incorporated into tutor advancement in rank and salary.

Areas of tutor performance that will be evaluated and by whom should be clearly stated during new-tutor training and updated with all tutors as needed. Program staff should also make clear the value given to each type of evaluation and how evaluation input is rewarded and/or addressed. In most circumstances, feedback from tutees is assumed to be the most important aspect of a tutor evaluation. Consistent favorable assessments from tutees would generally support continued employment. Consistent unfavorable assessments would support remediation of tutoring or subject area skills and/or termination of employment. What position does program staff take when a tutor receives favorable feedback from tutees but receives negative assessments from staff and other student employees? A tutor who is well-liked by tutees may fail to attend on-going training sessions and may not follow procedures for turning in timesheets and other important paperwork. If the tutor's behavior causes problems for other employees, it may be serious enough to terminate the tutor's employment. Program staff must explore responses to inconsistent evaluations and provide information and guidance to tutors. Presenting evaluation scenarios and discussing them with tutors during training helps to make expectations clear.

Faculty and non-program staff members who refer students to tutoring services may also provide feedback on tutor performance. This level of feedback can be formal or informal depending on referral procedures. If advisors, for example, use a formal referral process to send students to tutoring services, those advisors should be asked to report on feedback they receive from the referred students. Usually, though, the feedback process is more informal with advisors and/or faculty members reporting information in a more casual and general manner. Program staff must determine the level of importance of this input and how it will be incorporated into internal tutor evaluations.

The frequency of tutor evaluations is best determined by the assignment and scheduling system the tutoring system uses. If tutees are assigned to meet with a specific tutor for a predetermined time period, it would be appropriate to schedule evaluations of the tutor by the tutee after the first several sessions and at the end of the time period. If tutees make appointments with any available tutor and schedule appointments as needed, scheduling regular evaluation periods during the academic term provides the best opportunity for regular feedback from tutees. Input from program staff will usually occur regularly as staff has contact with tutors and tutees. Scheduling a formal evaluation session conducted by program staff each academic term, especially for new tutors, provides the opportunity for tutors to receive feedback from those who best understand tutor expectations and who make decisions about continued employment.

The rules of confidentiality that apply to employees also apply to tutor evaluations. Only those persons who legitimately need job performance information should have access to the evaluations; for example, for making decisions about continued employment and/or promotion, for solving problems identified through the process, or for making employment or educational references. Tutors being evaluated should receive a summary of evaluation input that does not identify individual evaluators. A compilation of all tutor evaluations from tutees can be used for comparing one tutor or one tutor group, such as new tutors, to the tutor group as a whole. However, the focus of tutor evaluations should be on individual progress from one evaluation period to the next. Tutors should be able to measure progress in specific assessment areas as they acquire experience and participate in advanced training.

PROGRAM SERVICES

Specific program services are tied to program philosophy, academic environment, and resources. Student needs should be assessed to determine the content of program services. Institutional research offices, admissions offices, and those responsible for undergraduate education at the institution can provide detailed demographics of the student population, as well as patterns of academic success. Students and faculty are also valuable sources of information on student needs. Most campuses have student outcomes-assessment programs that can provide valuable information on the achievement of and deficiencies in academic skills for identified segments of the student population.

One-on-one tutoring assistance is the primary focus of tutoring programs. The details of that service must be tied to program philosophy. Two important considerations are the length and frequency of tutoring sessions. Learning theory indicates that comprehension is tied to concentration and that high levels of concentration can be sustained for finite time periods. Tutoring sessions should be designed to maximize tutee concentration and scheduled for reasonable time periods, usually one-hour sessions. The number of times that tutees can meet with tutors is determined by the expectation of tutee independence and by the role of the tutor. If the program philosophy places tutors in the role of teachers, tutees and tutors may be able to meet as often as tutees determine is necessary. However, if program philosophy places tutors in the role of guides, tutees and tutors may be able to meet as often as the program staff has determined is reasonable to assure tutee independence. For example, tutees may be able to meet with tutors a certain number of times or for a certain amount of time each week. Exceptions can be made by tutor request.

Program philosophy may also dictate that the academic areas studied and the tutee's progress will determine the number and length of tutoring sessions. For example, if a student is meeting with a tutor to discuss a non-course-related topic such textbook reading strategies, the tutor and tutee may meet every day for a week until the tutee has mastered that strategy. However, a student enrolled in a mathematics class may only be able to meet with a tutor two or three times per week because it is assumed that the student should rely on class attendance as the primary source of course content. Program philosophy may dictate that tutees should not rely on tutors to replace class attendance.

Program philosophy can also help determine when tutoring services are offered during the academic term. Are services offered during the first week of classes, or are students expected to attend class for a week before engaging tutoring services? Are services offered during final examination week? Program philosophy can also determine approaches to specific tutoring content. Will tutors proofread papers or check accuracy of citations? Will tutors check homework assignments? Will tutors do research for tutees? Program philosophy determines whether or not tutors provide those services or teach tutees how to perform those operations themselves.

Although one-on-one tutoring is the primary focus of tutoring services, tutors may also work with students in group settings such as drop-in laboratories, workshops, and study groups. Tutors might also assist students in a computer laboratory setting where students work independently, seeking assistance when they encounter problems. Training sessions are expanded to incorporate these additional learning situations, keeping the core principles of one-on-one tutoring as the basis of these other tutoring services.

As we noted previously in this chapter, the predominant philosophies and theories of adult learning incorporate principles of learner independence to foster lifelong learning. This focus should be evident in the services offered by a tutoring program. Guidelines and practices that allow tutees to become dependent on tutors for academic success are opposed to lifelong learning development. A clear statement of philosophy and an effective training program are essential for ensuring that services focus appropriately on tutee learning and not on tutor expertise.

PROGRAM EVALUATION

The tutoring program should be evaluated regularly to ensure that services are meeting the needs of students and that the policies and procedures are consistent with the stated program philosophy and goals. Regular needs assessments are important even after tutoring programs are well established. As admission standards, core curricula, graduation requirements, and other academic rules change, needs assessments keep program services in line with the institution's academic environment. Needs assessments as part of program evaluation are also important if services must be put in priority order because of limited resources. Spending money wisely and allocating personnel to areas of greatest need are important elements of program success.

Tutees, tutors, other student employees, faculty, and non-program staff who make referrals to the program should take part in program evaluation activities. Program evaluations do not focus on individual tutors but rather on services. For example, tutees could be asked to assess satisfaction with services in general, efficiency of scheduling procedures, availability of reliable information about services, convenience of location and hours of operation, and assessment of policies. Tutors and other student employees can assess effectiveness of internal communication, quality of training programs, and efficacy of supervision. Faculty and non-program staff can assess effectiveness of external communication, including the availability of program service information, responsiveness to inquiries and referrals, and timeliness of communication.

In addition to evaluating current services, program evaluators can be asked to comment on additional needed services and to suggest service improvements. Tutors and other student employees can provide suggestions on internal communication and training programs. Faculty and non-program staff can offer ideas for improved external communication channels and for new services. Program evaluators often possess anecdotal information that can clearly describe evidence of both success and shortcomings. Evaluations from tutees and from faculty and non-program staff may be particularly important when new services are introduced. In fact, an evaluation process focusing only on a new service is an effective strategy when evaluators have provided consistent feedback on established services.

Program evaluation systems are most effective when there is a focus to the evaluation and when evaluators see results of the process. Evaluation questions focused on new services or previously identified weaknesses tend to elicit specific information that can be used to solve problems or enhance aspects of the service. Evaluation questions that focus on services in general may not provide more than a broad overview of levels of satisfaction and may not provoke specific comments. Summaries of program evaluations should be distributed to evaluators; changes that result from that evaluation input should be attributed to evaluators.

REFERENCES

Bergevin, Paul. 1967. *A philosophy for adult education.* New York: Seabury Press.

Casazza, Martha E., and Sharon L. Silverman. 1996. *Learning assistance and developmental education: A guide for effective practice.* San Francisco: Jossey-Bass.

White, Barbara, and Ralph Brockett. 1987. Putting philosophy into practice: Developing a working philosophy. *Journal of Extension* 25 (Summer): 11–14.

Zinn, Lorraine. 1990. Identifying your philosophical orientation. Chapter 3 in *Adult learning methods*, edited by Michael W. Griffith. Malabar, Fla.: Robert E. Krieger Publishing Company.

ADDITIONAL READINGS

Bruner, Jerome. 1960. *The process of education.* Cambridge, Mass.: Harvard University Press.

———. 1966. *On knowing: Essays for the left hand.* New York: Antheneum.

Kolb, David. 1983. *Experiential learning: Experience as the source of learning and development.* Englewood Cliffs, N.J.: Prentice-Hall.

McCarthy, Bernice. 1996. *About learning.* Barrington, Ill.: Excel.

Chapter 4

Establishing a Library Instruction Peer Tutoring Program

A Library Instruction Peer Tutoring Program (LITP) will most likely evolve from librarians, learning center staff, and/or tutors who recognize the need for research skills training through the application of peer assistance. Student-to-student learning is evident throughout the campus community. Particularly notable in the library are students working in small study groups, friends helping friends locate information, and strangers helping strangers at computer workstations. It is not uncommon to see students asking other students for help with computer applications and selection and use of databases in reference areas. Students routinely work together to complete research and other library-related assignments. Formalizing these peer interactions by establishing an LITP results in knowledgeable tutors trained in tutoring and research strategies. The benefits to students include reliable and accurate information, a supportive and non-threatening learning environment, and opportunities for guided practice.

When there is a lot of enthusiasm for establishing a new program, a common mistake is to just jump in and do it. However, the complexity of an LITP can rapidly show the folly of rushing in. Failing to give serious consideration to the program structure and foregoing methodical planning could cause the LITP to suffer from unnecessary growing pains. In this chapter, we offer an approach to planning for a new LITP by discussing possible collaborations in terms of program structure, by identifying components of the planning process, and by offering considerations for implementation.

PROGRAM STRUCTURE

Before planning for an LITP, one important question regarding program structure must be answered: Should the program be established through collaboration with an existing campus learning center or should it be a library-based program? Compatibility of the mission and goals of the library and learning center with support from administrators is essential for a successful collaborative program.

Most post-secondary institutions provide tutoring services for students. Many two-year, post-secondary institutions have a learning resource center that combines library resources with academic support services. Even in two-year institutions that do not use that model, numerous tutoring services are usually available, either through a centralized learning center or through specific department programs. It is not unusual for the English Department, for example, to support student learning through a writing lab or for the Math Department to provide math tutoring. In four-year institutions, tutoring services may be available to students in specific academic programs, through centralized learning centers, and/or through department-based services.

Established tutoring programs will have in place the elements we described in the previous chapter: mechanisms for recruiting and hiring tutors, training tutors, and evaluating tutors and programs. Most programs provide assistance for students enrolled in specific courses. Some programs may provide tutoring for study strategies, either exclusively or as a complement to course specific tutoring. Library instruction tutoring can easily be organized as a stand-alone subject area such as math, English, or physics, or as a component of study-strategies tutoring. Study-strategies tutoring usually includes student behaviors related to academic success such as textbook reading, time management, test taking, listening, and note taking.

Most established tutoring programs do not currently provide library instruction tutoring because they lack tutor and/or staff expertise in teaching library-information-research skills. Many tutoring programs hire tutors based on their grades in specific courses in the subject area that will be tutored. There are very few library science courses in which potential library instruction tutors can enroll as a prerequisite for tutoring. Within these traditional tutoring programs the expertise is not available for providing the needed training for library instruction tutors or for determining the curriculum of a library instruction tutoring program.

Librarians possess the expertise for determining the tutoring curriculum and providing the training. However, they lack the expertise to establish a tutoring program. Library-based tutoring services require the infrastructure that most established tutoring programs presuppose. Although content knowledge is easily found among library staff, creating the elements of a successful tutoring program might seem overwhelming, especially for an already busy Reference or Instruction Department. Collaboration between the library and established campus tutoring programs can be the basis for program structure.

Numerous possibilities exist for collaboration when library and learning center missions, goals, and values are congruent. On those campuses with centralized tutoring programs, we suggest that using the tutoring program infrastructure for the library instruction tutoring program is an effective approach. The model detailed in this book uses the collaborative approach to an LITP. Working together, a librarian and a learning center's program coordinator can determine the requisite academic background and interpersonal skills needed for a library instruction tutor position. Tutors can be recruited from among student employees in the library and from students who can demonstrate the requisite research and library use skills. A librarian can create a curriculum for tutoring sessions and for the training program that supports that curriculum. The librarian-created component becomes the content training unit for the library instruction tutors in much the same way a professor determines course content. An established program will have routine monitoring and evaluation measures that can be extended to library instruction tutoring. The location of library instruction tutoring can be negotiated based on available space and resources. Tutoring programs certified by the CRLA meet specific guidelines for recruiting, selecting, and hiring tutors; for training tutors at new, regular, advanced, and master levels; and for evaluating tutors. For a list of institutions with CRLA-certified tutor training programs, see Appendix A.

On campuses without a centralized tutoring program, a writing center or a study strategies program provides content that can be closely tied to library instruction. Again, the infrastructure of those programs can provide the organization for a library instruction tutoring program. If there is no appropriate tutoring program with which to collaborate, a library-based program can be created. The foundations of a peer tutoring program, as outlined in the previous chapter, can serve as the structure for a library-based LITP. Most likely, library-based tutoring services would be an extension of library instruction or reference services.

Exploring program structure possibilities as a preliminary step to the planning process creates the opportunity to shape planning efforts around program design. If an existing tutoring program becomes the context for a library instruction tutoring program, the planning process does not have to include organizational design. If a library-based program is created, the planning process will have to include the organization of a tutoring program.

PLANNING

Program planning is the process of establishing priorities, identifying potential problems, and allocating resources to achieve goals and objectives. One of the frustrations many people express about program planning is that it never seems to end. This is true. Planning needs to be kept alive in organizations for two reasons: (1) knowledge and experience gained from practice should always be fed back into the planning process to keep the program responsive to the needs it is designed to serve; and (2) communities change, the information environment changes, and peoples' needs change. Information needs of students in the year 2000 and the resources available to meet those needs may not be the same two, five, or ten years from now. For these reasons, it is wise to set up a strong foundation for planning and foster enthusiasm for the process from the very beginning.

A pilot project is an effective planning and implementation tool. It allows a program to be implemented on a small scale and provides feedback into the planning process. When the pilot project is complete, decisions about establishing and implementing the program can be reviewed, modified, and finalized. We recommend undertaking a pilot project when considering the creation of an LITP. The information in this chapter can be used as a guide for launching a pilot project as part of the planning and implementation process.

Needs Assessment

The first step in planning a program is to conduct a needs assessment by examining the overall mission and goals of the campus learning center and the campus library. Collaboration may be wanted and necessary to implement an LITP.

The following may be helpful in conducting a needs assessment.

- Do library users express a need for library instruction tutoring, and how likely would they be to use LITP services? Conduct a user survey to identify needs and determine potential use.

- What are the reference questions, lasting more than five or ten minutes, which require in-depth instruction? Observe Reference Desk interactions and query reference personnel.

- Is the existing library instruction program meeting the individual training needs of students? Analyze library instruction session evaluations completed by students and query instruction personnel to identify individualized instruction needs.

- Are introductory students coming to the academic institution with strong backgrounds in performing library research? Survey students in introductory courses and/or new student orientations.

Student Input Survey

To assess the need for implementing an LITP, a sample survey can be given to current tutees and tutors of the campus learning center. The survey gathers information from students who are already familiar with using tutoring services and may become potential users of the LITP. (See Appendix B for a sample survey.) The Student Input Survey can also help to define possible future users and identify a target audience for the service. Defining an appropriate target group for the LITP is vital for determining the tutoring session content and creating the tutor training curriculum.

The Student Input Survey would most likely include questions on demographics, current patterns of library use, and levels of interest in potentially using library-instruction-tutoring services. The demographic information needed depends on the existing knowledge of the survey group. Questions about current patterns of library use may include library services currently used, frequency of use, and areas in which students desire more training. Potential use of LITP services can be determined by asking if library-instruction-tutoring sessions would have been helpful in the past and how likely students are to use library instruction tutoring in the future.

The LITP can benefit new and continuing students. The survey should be distributed to groups of beginning freshmen, returning and transfer students, and new graduate students. This survey audience may profit from the services if they are unfamiliar with the campus library system, have limited skills in searching databases, or need a refresher on basic research skills.

Training Curriculum and Session Content Input

To determine what information should be covered in library-instruction-tutoring sessions, input is needed from library faculty and staff, students who currently participate in library instruction sessions, and students who participate in orientation programs and introductory courses. The information gained is used to determine the content of tutoring sessions and is also used to create the tutor training curriculum.

➤ Solicit Input from Library Faculty and Staff

When determining the appropriate scope for the LITP, it is best to begin with the experts in the field and in the subject area; for this program, then, it is important to address and gather information from library faculty, staff, and students. This process should involve faculty and staff from as many areas of the library as possible. Obviously, reference personnel have direct knowledge of students' needs because they see students on a day-to-day basis and are familiar with typical questions and requests for assistance. Also important are the people who develop and maintain information database systems. Personnel in technical services and library technology departments have expert knowledge and can contribute to the survey.

If a program within a large organization is to be successful, people need to feel that they are a part of it. Involving as many departments, branches, and personnel as possible can only enhance the success of the program. Representation from the following library areas is advisable: reference, circulation, interlibrary loan, catalog or technical services departments, government information, and special collections.

Input from library personnel will provide a foundation for the tutoring session content and the tutor training curriculum. There are no wrong propositions, and all input is valuable. Survey questions might include open-ended questions such as: "What library strategies and skills does a new student need to be a successful researcher at our institution?" and "What strategies and skills can be learned through peer tutoring?" Discussion meetings are encouraged; brainstorming techniques can be used to solicit the widest range of ideas and suggestions.

The comments may vary from department to department. Suggestions from the circulation department staff may include the importance of general circulation policies including fines and billing procedures, loan periods, use of reserve items, services such as recalling books and photocopying, and information on library tours and other public services. Reference personnel may comment on defining what an on-line catalog is and what it is not, hours of operation, recognizing call numbers and finding the items, using electronic and paper resources, accessing the library from home, and implementing search strategies. The catalog and/or technical services personnel may point out the importance of record structure, subject versus keyword searching, vocabulary, and database configuration. All these suggestions are valid and will help define the focus of LITP services and training.

During these survey sessions, an overview of peer tutoring expectations and services and explorations of collaboration can be presented and discussed. An LITP provides a new level of library instruction assistance, meeting needs for individualized instruction and complementing current reference services and instruction programs. By applying a collaborative model, the library provides expertise for training and tutoring curricula. In designing the training curriculum, the library plays the role of the professor in the classroom. The tutoring session content helps to establish boundaries and allows tutors to make proper referrals. Tutoring content does not replace reference services or instruction programs, but better prepares the tutees to request information and conduct research.

➤ *Analyze Instruction Session Evaluations*

Most library instruction programs have session evaluations as a component of course-related sessions and database workshops. These evaluations result in input about the specific session and often include a comment section. Student responses offer valuable information about the need for a tutoring program and the design of tutor training curriculum.

Potential users of a peer tutoring program may list the following concerns: the pace of the session was too fast, more hands-on and practice time was needed, computer skills were inadequate, users were unsure of the next steps for finding material, and the users needed more individual attention. These responses indicate the students' need for focused, one-on-one tutoring sessions. During these sessions, the tutor and tutee can set an appropriate pace to ensure that the student comprehends the concepts and processes. Library instruction personnel can also provide information concerning the need for more individualized instruction based on their observations and interactions with students during instruction sessions.

➤ *Survey Students in Introductory*
 Courses/Orientations

Surveying students in mandatory and/or large-enrollment, freshman-level courses can provide an assessment of their library research skills. Survey questions could include assessments of database searching knowledge, research strategies, critical thinking levels, and prior library usage. An effective survey would include applications of knowledge to research scenarios. For example, a question requiring students to outline research strategies for a course-related topic, to choose appropriate databases for the topic, and to identify selected fields in records provides information concerning proficiency in library research skills. Faculty members who teach these courses can also supply input on student proficiencies.

Other avenues for gathering student information are orientation programs for new students—freshmen, transfers, and graduates. Survey questions should be adapted and appropriate to the expected research skill levels of each student group. Orientation programs are made up of large numbers of survey participants who represent a wide range of academic backgrounds and interests. For those reasons, orientation surveys cannot be as focused as course-related surveys. Most orientations are held throughout the summer months, prior to the beginning of the academic year. This scheduling provides the opportunity for early needs assessment for incoming students.

Analysis of Needs Assessment

Input from the needs assessment process will determine the viability of a peer tutoring approach to library instruction. Students must indicate a desire for more instruction time and for individualized instruction; teaching faculty must recognize the need for improved student research skills; and library faculty and staff must incorporate peer tutoring as a viable tool in the learning of library research. At this time, program structure decisions can be made and planning for implementation can begin.

CONSIDERATIONS FOR IMPLEMENTATION

Basic considerations for implementation include responsibilities of collaboration between the library and the learning center, human resources needs, operational needs, and development of a pilot project. A thorough examination of these considerations is essential to effective implementation.

Responsibilities of Collaboration

The collaborative model presupposes the use of the learning center infrastructure for program organization. The learning center has policies and procedures for recruiting, hiring, and evaluating tutors, along with an established tutor training program. Training program components include interpersonal communication skills, tutoring strategies, appropriate boundaries, ethics, confidentiality, learning styles, professionalism, subject area content, and policies and procedures. Working together, library and learning center personnel can determine the criteria for hiring library instruction tutors. Library instruction will be considered a separate subject area, and the library-instruction-training curriculum will be incorporated into the existing tutor training structure for the subject area. The model assumes that the library will provide the subject expertise for the content of library instruction tutor training and will determine the content of tutoring sessions. The learning center will provide the organizational structure and daily supervision of tutors.

Human Resources

Learning center and library staff will participate in a variety of ways when library instruction tutoring is provided. They will identify potential tutors, conduct training sessions, promote the program, make referrals, identify resources, and participate in program evaluation. The most important responsibilities, though, will be assigned to a coordinator who guarantees that the tutors receive the training and support they need to successfully provide services to students.

Library Instruction Tutor Coordinator Responsibilities

The Library Instruction Tutor Coordinator (LITC) is responsible for defining the curriculum, for serving as a liaison between the library and the campus learning center, and for overseeing the initial and on-going training of library instruction tutors. This professional librarian position provides leadership and is responsible for program development. Duties include gathering input for the training curriculum from each library public and technical service area, including reference departments of all branches, interlibrary loan, circulation, copy services, cataloging, and others. The LITC analyzes the data gathered based on suggestions from library personnel. After a detailed analysis of all data collected, patterns and overlapping ideas become apparent and create the library instruction tutor training curriculum that will support the actual tutoring sessions.

After the tutoring session content has been established, the training program for the tutors is developed. The training program incorporates the curriculum basics into hands-on applications. The LITC can serve as the subject area team leader during the pilot project, provide initial and ongoing training, and supervise the tutors.

Another important aspect of the LITC's responsibilities will be participation with the campus learning center managers. Although the campus learning center has a process for hiring tutors, the LITC will be actively involved in hiring library instruction tutors. The LITC will need to become an expert on the organizational structure and internal mechanisms of the learning center. Learning center managers will supply information and support for integrating the library instruction program into learning center services. As the subject area team leader, the LITC may have other administrative duties during the pilot project: for example, coordinating library instruction tutoring schedules, conducting regular tutor group meetings, participating in team leader activities, and communicating regularly with learning center managers.

Tutor Duties and Responsibilities

Library instruction tutors are responsible for knowing the content of their area and for knowing general tutoring strategies. Tutors are responsible for helping tutees gain knowledge and skills in library policies and resources, research strategies, database searching, and locating and evaluating information. Tutors direct tutees in the development of these skills so that tutees become independent learners. Tutors do not perform research for tutees, but rather guide tutees through the research process.

An important aspect of tutor training is the understanding and setting of boundaries in the tutoring relationship. In addition to the expectations and boundaries discussed in Chapter 3, library instruction tutors are faced with the challenge of avoiding becoming amateur reference librarians. The content of tutoring is limited to basic skills performed in the research process and does not include specific subject area expertise. Tutors are expected to make appropriate referrals to other library services. For example, tutors can assist tutees in accessing reference services by identifying when it is appropriate to request reference assistance, by helping to overcome the fear of asking for assistance, and by using the appropriate language to frame a reference question.

A crucial responsibility of library instruction tutors is to create a tutoring environment that focuses on the tutee's application and demonstration of research skills. Tutees are not just shown or told how to perform research, but are actively engaged in the research process. Tutor training curriculum must contain active learning strategies that can be used during tutoring sessions. Appropriate questioning can structure the tutoring session to reinforce current research skills and to introduce and gain new abilities. Answers to questions can provide feedback to the tutor and tutee about progress made in acquiring research skills and developing independent application of the research process. For example, rather than telling or showing a tutee how to e-mail a citation from a specific database, the tutor would ask questions that help the tutee interpret the commands that would allow the tutee to e-mail the citation. As the tutee executes the commands, the tutor observes and provides feedback as needed.

During a typical tutoring session, the tutor is responsible for determining the tutee's previous research experience, assessing current skills levels and research needs, offering instruction on research approaches and specific research tools, and incorporating a review of the tutoring session content. Previous research experience can easily be determined with a short student survey during the initial library instruction tutoring session (see Appendix B). An initial survey could include, for example, questions on library use patterns, use of specific library services and resources, experience with various classification schemes, and identification of commonly used library terms. Based on the initial survey, the tutor can quickly determine current skills levels. The tutor can query the tutee on specific research needs. Research needs can be as varied as finding books and articles for a research paper or project to learning basic computer search methods. The tutor may propose a series of tutoring sessions to build needed library research skills. When providing instruction, the tutor adapts the library instruction curriculum to meet the specific research needs and skills level of the tutee. Relying on information provided by the tutee and on the tutor's own training and experience in library research, the tutor selects a library resource and introduces the resource at an appropriate skill level. At the conclusion of the tutoring session, the tutor will have the tutee review and demonstrate learned skills and will encourage the practice of these skills before any scheduled follow-up tutoring sessions.

As discussed in Chapter 3, tutors are also expected to follow program policies and procedures and to participate in all required training sessions. Library instruction tutors must also recognize the nature of working in a collaborative program. Tutors must be flexible and understand the different roles of the LITC and the learning center program supervisor. The LITC provides content information and initial and on-going training for library research skills. The learning center provides initial and on-going training in tutoring principles and supervises the daily activities of library instruction tutors including scheduling, payroll, supplies and materials, and evaluations. Library instruction tutoring will be integrated into learning center services. The learning center provides a supportive work environment by assessing additional training needs, providing opportunities for personal and professional development, and assisting with personnel and other job-related issues.

Recruiting and Hiring Library Instruction Tutors

The successful recruitment and hiring of the first group of library instruction tutors is essential for implementing a new LITP. Questions regarding qualifications, recruitment strategies, and scalability must be answered for successful implementation.

Recruiting can only begin once the required and preferred qualifications are determined. A sample of the required skills for library instruction tutors could be an overall grade point average of 3.0 or higher, along with good communication, organizational, and interpersonal skills. Preferred qualities include a background in computers, prior tutoring experience, and experience in performing library research, either from an introductory library research class or an assigned research paper from a subject course. Applicants must also include references with at least one recommendation from a faculty member. Unofficial transcripts will also need to accompany the application. (See Appendix A for CRLA requirements.)

Library instruction tutors need to have excellent interpersonal and listening skills. Tutoring others requires a great deal of patience and understanding, especially with tutees who have limited research skills. Tutors must also have a demonstrated interest in computer technology and the desire to help others with research.

Once the required and preferred qualifications are established, a publicity campaign can be implemented. Learning centers have established procedures for advertising student positions that can now include library instruction tutors. Recruitment of students may begin by advertising in the campus newspaper and on relevant Web pages. Sending notices of the job description to faculty and departments also helps to get the word out. During the pilot project phase, additional recruitment measures may be needed. For example, the LITC can recruit potential tutors from undergraduate and graduate library science courses as well as courses that require research papers.

Because the skills needed for library instruction tutors are not discipline specific, one of the best recruiting methods may be to approach students applying for other tutoring positions. For example, the applicant pool for linguistics or English tutors may contain a number of qualified students in those areas. However, the number of qualified applicants may exceed the number of available positions. There may be excellent library instruction tutor candidates within those pools who may be interested in a library instruction tutoring position.

Current library student employees make up another pool of potential library instruction tutor candidates. Their work in the library has given these students knowledge and skills in organizing and accessing information. Library training may have covered call number systems, material formats and locations, electronic resources, and policies and procedures. Library student employees often shelve materials, check materials in and out, process new acquisitions, and provide directional and collection assistance to library patrons. These acquired skills are a practical foundation for the knowledge needed in library instruction tutoring positions. In fact, new library instruction tutors who lack previous library experience might benefit from participating in library student employee training.

Goals, Considerations, and Evaluation of a Pilot Project

Establishing the collaborative model, identifying the LITC, determining tutoring and training curricula, and recruiting and hiring tutors are the basic elements of program implementation that provide the core for a pilot project. The pilot project offers the opportunity to implement program services on a small scale for a predetermined period of time such as an academic term or year. The needs assessment profiles from the planning process will indicate the potential audience and demand for library instruction tutoring services. The learning center can provide information on previous implementation patterns for new tutoring programs. With this information, pilot project targets for scalability of tutors and tutees can be estimated.

Core Goals of the Pilot Project

One goal of a pilot project is to integrate the LITP into learning center services. By incorporating library instruction tutoring into existing campus tutoring services, tutees can receive assistance with research skills through the same system they use to access other academic support services. Tutees will recognize library instruction as an academic area in which they can improve their skills through peer assistance. Library instruction tutors benefit from integration into the learning center by having the opportunity to share tutoring experiences, learn from tutors in other subject areas, and enhance tutee learning in academic areas where research is performed. Library instruction tutors may work in tandem with other tutors in subject areas such as education, humanities, social sciences, English, reading, or other areas requiring research.

Another goal of the pilot project is to increase the awareness of learning center services within the library. Learning center personnel and the LITC can make presentations to appropriate library groups explaining the program philosophy, structure, and services. Tutor hiring, training, expectations, and evaluations should be thoroughly described. The LITC plays a pivotal role in building a new partnership between the library and the learning center. By involving library personnel in tutoring and training curriculum development, the LITC helps develop library-wide understanding of the collaborative relationship between the library and learning center.

Another goal of the pilot project is to provide services. Tutoring services often include one-on-one appointments, drop-in labs, and small-group instruction. A successful pilot project will focus on one particular service format. The recommended focus for a pilot project is one-on-one tutoring. Training is then adjusted to meet the needs of the tutors in one-on-one relationships with tutees. This format most readily identifies and limits tutoring content, focuses specifically on the skill level and research needs of the tutee, and assists the tutor in developing interpersonal tutoring skills. Drop-in lab and small-group instruction services may evolve from a strong one-on-one tutoring program, but are not generally provided by new or regular tutors. Advanced training is required for working with groups of tutees in workshop or drop-in lab scenarios.

Considerations for a Pilot Project

Location and equipment, resources, and promotional strategies are elements to consider before implementing a pilot project. Aspects of each element will involve cooperation from and collaboration between the library and learning center. Costs for new equipment, supplies and materials, and advertising should be incorporated into the collaborative agreement between the library and learning center.

During the pilot project, library instruction tutors should be located within the learning center, preferably in a highly visible area. The new library instruction tutoring services will be easily accessible to tutees who currently use other learning center services. The inclusion of the LITP in the learning center facilitates appointment scheduling; access to learning center personnel, including other tutors; and participation in established tutor and program evaluation processes. The climate of peer assistance at the learning center allows tutees to experience library instruction in a familiar format and environment.

Library instruction tutors need appropriate hardware and software to access library resources. The minimal workstation hardware includes a computer with Ethernet or dial-up connections. Additional workstation features that may enhance the tutoring session include a printer and sound capability. Minimal workstation software includes a Web browser, e-mail access, and Telnet connections. Additional software can include word processing, spreadsheets, and/or database management applications. The number of tutors scheduled during any particular time period determines the number of workstations required. Equipment configuration should be similar to that found in the library and/or campus computer labs so that tutees can easily apply learned skills in various environments. Adequate workspace for the tutor and tutee that is in compliance with the Americans with Disabilities Act is also necessary.

Within the tutoring work area, tutors need specific library tools such as the Library of Congress subject headings, database-specific thesauri, and dictionaries. In addition, library and training materials that contain library and learning center policies and procedures, tutoring guidelines and strategies, and library instruction guides are needed. Some materials are designed for tutor training and development; others are used during tutoring sessions and can be distributed to the tutees.

During the pilot project, the promotion of the new library instruction tutoring services should be directed to the audiences identified during the planning process. Passive marketing strategies include advertisements in campus publications, fliers and brochures, and signage within the library and learning center. In a more active strategy, library instruction tutors can make presentations that promote the new services to students enrolled in courses requiring library research, as well as to other student groups expressing interest. Another active strategy is to educate library personnel and other tutors on making appropriate referrals to library instruction tutoring services. An orientation for library personnel should be held at the learning center at the beginning of the pilot project and should include learning center policies and procedures as well as an overview of library instruction tutoring content. Subject area tutoring in research-related disciplines can be strengthened through appropriate referrals to library instruction tutors. Subject area tutors often identify and recognize tutee deficiencies in research strategies; they can now refer those students to the new library instruction tutoring service.

Evaluation of the Pilot Project

The pilot project is an essential phase in the implementation process, providing the opportunity for examination of the LITP. When the pilot project is complete, tutors, the LITC, other library personnel, and learning center staff evaluate all aspects of the LITP pilot project. Tutors can provide suggestions for improvements on hiring criteria; tutoring and library instruction training curricula; adequacy of workspace, equipment, and resources; and tutoring session content. Tutors can also gather and report information on how frequently tutees use the library and its services, their knowledge of research and related skills levels, and on the tutees' specific research needs. This information can be compared to the profile of potential users created during the needs assessment to determine the profile of actual users. If the profiles differ significantly, changes in implementation may be necessary.

The LITC and other library personnel can assess the quality of the library instruction training curriculum and tutoring session content based upon feedback from the tutors and library trainers. Library personnel may have feedback regarding interactions with students who worked with library instruction tutors. They may also have suggestions for promotion strategies for referring students to library instruction tutoring services.

Learning center staff can provide actual tutee feedback from tutor and program evaluation processes on tutoring skills and quality of services. They can also assess the quality of the tutor training curriculum and the requisites for hiring based upon input from the library instruction tutors. Learning center staff can also evaluate usage patterns for future scheduling and the number of tutors needed for full program implementation.

Three possible outcomes of the LITP pilot project evaluation are (1) choosing not to implement an LITP, (2) significantly modifying the LITP and piloting a revised program, or (3) implementing the LITP. A decision not to implement the program would most likely be based on feedback that the program did not meet the needs of students or a lack of financial and/or human resources. Information gained from the pilot project could be used to improve learning center services and library instruction programs even if the specific pilot project did not meet the needs of students. If resources are lacking, information from the pilot project could be used to seek funding for program implementation in the future.

The strengths and weaknesses identified through the evaluation process may result in significant changes to the LITP as originally designed and may include a second pilot project. If the program met the research needs of the tutees, implementation should be seriously considered. However, if other program aspects did not work well for tutees, tutors, library personnel, and/or learning center staff, the LITP plan must be revised to address those program aspects. Significant changes might include physically relocating the program to the library, changing the format of tutoring from one-on-one appointments to drop-in lab or group instruction, and/or changing the collaborative agreement in the areas of supervision and coordination. These changes would warrant a revised LITP plan that includes a new pilot project.

If the pilot project evaluation resulted in a positive assessment from tutees, tutors, library personnel, and learning center staff, the commitment to implement the program on a continuing basis can be made. The collaborative agreement between the library and learning center can be finalized with responsibilities for resources, hiring, training, supervision, and evaluation clearly identified. The successful pilot project becomes the basis for implementation. The continual planning process will result in future improvements and possible program expansions.

A key element of developing an LITP is a sound tutor training curriculum. No pilot project will be successful without a training curriculum that empowers tutors with the knowledge of the content area and with the skills to effectively interact with tutees. The library instruction tutoring content must be understood at the conceptual level before it can be effectively applied in a tutoring session. The library is responsible for the development of and training in library content. The learning center is responsible for the development of and training in tutoring concepts and skills. This collaboration is the foundation of an LITP. A model of an LITP conceptual training curriculum is presented in Chapter 5.

Chapter 5

Conceptual Curriculum for Library Instruction Tutor Program

Teaching faculty design and develop the course curriculum that provides the content for subject area tutoring. The tutors have taken courses within a particular discipline, giving them a substantial knowledge of a subject area. They provide assistance by helping students process, understand, and retain the course content. On most campuses, students do not have the opportunity to take credit courses that allow them to gain a substantial knowledge of the library research process. The challenge for an LITP is to develop a tutor training curriculum that generates the content for library instruction tutoring. The major curriculum concepts include a history of information storage and retrieval, the organization of information, research strategies, components of electronic searching, and the evaluation of information. These concepts provide a framework for training tutors and do not necessarily reflect the content of tutoring sessions.

The training curriculum is centered on technological advances that have dramatically changed the way we perform research and access information. Researchers can now connect to libraries and research centers from their homes or offices with a computer and a telephone line. These electronic advances have made accessing resources easier, but have also required learning new skills and concepts. Conducting research appears easy to those who have mastered the art of researching, but to the novice it may appear so ominous that even the feeblest attempt can cause feelings of frustration, anger, and inadequacy. According to *TechnoStress* authors, "85% to 90% of the population is not eagerly embracing technology" (Weil and Rosen 1997, 22). Even though libraries have entered the Information Age quite rapidly, a great proportion of the population has been left behind. As librarians and educators, it is our responsibility to offer humanistic learning situations that will enable students to acquire the knowledge and skills to perform effective library research. Weil and Rosen suggest that those who need assistance in learning technology get a "personal trainer" (1997, 45). Library instruction tutors are personal trainers for students who need to find information. Understanding the history of information storage and retrieval supplies the background and context for the process of performing research.

HISTORY OF ACCESSING INFORMATION

Information storage and retrieval has been around for thousands of years. Humans, by nature, want to record and preserve history for future generations. Only the materials and storage units have changed throughout time. As each society becomes more sophisticated in its recording methods, it acquires knowledge that leads it to the appropriate information storage method. The process of retrieving recorded information evolves as well. After acquiring and recording knowledge, systematic techniques for retrieving bits of information are needed. Indexes, card catalogs, and lists assisted the users in finding detailed information. Major leaps in information storage and retrieval have been made over the centuries through the use of technology.

Cave Walls to Personal Computers

The earliest recorded representation of *Homo sapiens* can be found on cave walls. Forty thousand years ago, humans were painting pictures to record events, using materials made of natural dyes. Cuneiform, an ancient Middle Eastern form of pictorial writing, began around 5,000 years ago. Pictures could capture the essence of the scene, but could not provide the needed representation of sound or language. The creation of the alphabet allowed symbols to represent sounds and led to recording systems based on written language.

Materials used in the earliest recording systems included bones, wood, stone, and baked clay tablets. As societies evolved, their desire for a more appropriate writing surface also evolved. Papyrus, vellum, and parchment came into use in the first millennium B.C. The first book, or codex, was invented by sewing together the edges of parchment, thus creating the first information storage unit. As the discovery of paper made its way west from China, the book came to be the preferred source for storing information.

Johann Gutenberg's use of the printing press in the 1450s allowed for the mass production of books, which made information more widely available. Books could be produced relatively quickly and uniformly and distributed in quantity. Literate societies began to use printing to record the history of language. It was not until the twentieth century that technology, first through steam and then through electricity, replaced typesetting and papermaking by hand.

The twentieth century saw the invention of radio and the motion picture. Television brought sound and moving pictures into each household in America. These revolutions only enhanced the recorded written word via different formats. The advent of the personal computer and telecommunication capabilities had a profound effect on society by providing global access to information including the written word, pictures, and sound.

Personal computers have enhanced the process of accessing, storing, and retrieving information. The computer has the capacity to store and retrieve large amounts of information on a microcomputer chip. Telecommunications capabilities allow computers around the world to communicate with each other.

These changes have revolutionized access to information. Society can now access information and perform research from home or office, 24 hours a day.

Gatekeepers to Gateways

During the 1970s, 1980s, and early 1990s, electronic databases were being developed and paper indexes were becoming available on-line. Librarians were the main gatekeepers of on-line searching. A typical on-line search would require the patron to make an appointment with a librarian or an on-line searcher to go over the specific concepts and details of a search. The librarian would help the student define concepts and vocabulary and would suggest appropriate databases. On-line searches also carried a fee depending on the amount of time spent on-line in the database and on how many citations were extracted. The librarian or on-line searcher had to be very proficient in his or her searching skills to reduce the cost to the student. Some database vendors allowed students to search databases independently of librarians at reduced costs and at special times. Short instruction courses were offered to familiarize the students with the concepts and commands of on-line searching. These short courses offered instruction on Boolean logic, vocabulary, database structure and content, and search commands. Again, the students using the systems were responsible for paying on-line charges.

The introduction of the CD-ROM provided electronic access to databases without the worry about time or money while searching. Again, short courses were offered at many institutions on the use of CD-ROM software. Students were responsible for searching on their own with little or no assistance. This new technology created the trend for students becoming their own gatekeepers of information.

The responsibility of knowing and understanding the concepts of searching was now transferred to the students. It was observed in many on-line search rooms that when students needed searching or computer assistance, they would often ask another student sitting nearby for help. Whether the question was a simple one dealing with printing citations or finding the right command to display abstracts, students would try to help other students. As students were taking on the role of gatekeepers and becoming more responsible for search techniques, technology was driving libraries to become gateways for electronic resources.

A knowledge of the development of information storage and retrieval systems and the impact of technology will assist tutors in understanding the tutees' responsibilities in conducting their own research. As tutees acquire independent research capabilities, the tutors serve as human gateways to the needed research skills. An understanding of this first concept provides a context for exploring how information is produced and organized.

ORGANIZATION OF INFORMATION

Tutors need to know the process of communication and the organization of information. The process of how information is created, published, distributed, acquired, and classified brings an understanding of how information is searched for and retrieved.

Communication begins with authors, writers, and editors who want to convey an opinion, idea, or a description to others. The communicator submits work for publication to a publisher who prints or reproduces the work in an appropriate format. The format could be a book, journal, magazine, newspaper, or video recording, for example. The publisher then makes the work available to the public or to a special interest group. Once the work has been published and distributed, it may be indexed to make the information retrievable. It is important to note that not all information produced is indexed. Indexing companies only index the information that they believe is important to potential users.

Libraries receive, catalog, and classify the information acquired. They make the retrieval of information available to their patrons through reference sources, encyclopedias, on-line and card catalogs, and indexes (paper and electronic). Most university libraries use the Library of Congress (LC) Classification System to organize their collections. The LC Classification System groups materials on similar topics together by subject. Libraries, though, may use more than one classification system for different collections. For example, government information departments use the Superintendent of Documents classification system, or SuDocs. The SuDoc system classifies U.S. government information by agencies and departments.

Knowing how information is created, classified, and organized assists tutors in understanding the strategies for accessing and retrieving information. Tutors will need to know which classification systems are used, for which collection, within the libraries. Knowledge of the locations of collections will help the tutors assist the tutees with finding materials. The curriculum for the tutors must also include the fundamental concepts of library research strategies and electronic searching.

RESEARCH STRATEGIES

Tutors help tutees to develop research strategies. Students select a topic after considering the assignment requirements, personal interests, availability of materials, and the time given to complete the assignment. Tutors go over the assignment with the tutee to assess appropriate research strategies. They also help to narrow or broaden the student's search by suggesting resources and making referrals to reference personnel. Performing research is a process, and following step-by-step guidelines can help simplify that process. It can be broken down into three basic strategies: current, factual, and traditional. Although there are many ways to perform research, we present these three strategies to help tutors develop an understanding of fundamental research approaches.

Current Topic Research Strategies

Current topics can be found in periodical and newspaper indexes and abstracts. If the topic is too recent to have been indexed, researchers can browse the table of contents of current periodicals to find articles on their topic. Bibliographies are sometimes included in articles and can be useful in finding related information. Other resources such as government publications or statistical sources can also provide relevant information. Searching the Web is a viable option as well. Current information on any topic can often be found on the Web within minutes of the reported event or release of news stories. Associations and organizations can also be explored by contacting them directly. By investigating these current topic resources, students can assess if the topic they have chosen is suitable for their paper or assignment.

Tutors must possess strategies for researching current topics. A current topic checklist provides a structured approach to accessing relevant resources. A current topic checklist may include:

- Newspaper indexes and abstracts
- Periodical indexes and abstracts
- Government publications
- Statistical resources
- Associations and organizations
- Bibliographies
- The Web
- A reference librarian.

Factual Research Strategy

Facts and statistics may be required to support data within a paper. Tutors need to consider what types of resources are available to find needed and related facts, and whether the fact is biographical, statistical, an address, a date, or a definition. Materials that may answer questions can be in a variety of resources such as dictionaries, encyclopedias, directories, or handbooks. More than one department within the library may house relevant factual information. When performing factual research, reference resources are often consulted first. Government information resources contain a wealth of local, state, federal, and international statistical data, covering a plethora of topics. When searching for factual information, tutors need to know not only the types of resources but where the resources are located. A factual research checklist may include:

- Encyclopedias

- Dictionaries

- Directories

- Handbooks

- Periodical indexes and abstracts

- The Web.

Traditional Research Strategies

When researching an in-depth topic, it is helpful to start with background information that provides an overview before narrowing the search focus. Encyclopedia articles help to define the major concepts of the topic as well as suggest subtopics and bibliographies. Books also provide background information and lead researchers to other resources through bibliographies. Periodical indexes and abstracts assist in focusing the topic and provide the most current information. A traditional research checklist may include:

- Encyclopedias

- On-line catalog

- Periodical/newspaper indexes and abstracts

- Statistical resources

- Book reviews.

Tutors must understand that there is no one right way to perform research. Often researchers happen upon information serendipitously. These fundamental search strategies are guidelines for places to begin the research process. Knowing these strategies gives tutors the information they need to select the appropriate research strategy and identify relevant resources.

COMPONENTS OF ELECTRONIC SEARCHING

Electronic searching includes several basic concepts. To search effectively, tutors will need to know how a database is structured, what the contents are, the importance of using the correct vocabulary, and the Boolean operators.

Database Structure

Determining what types of databases exist and how they are structured is fundamental to understanding and searching computerized resources. Tutors do not have to be computer programmers, but understanding the structure of databases and how computers search for information helps them to become effective searchers.

Databases consist of records that are made up of a number of fields. Fields have labels and contain information such as au: author, ti: title, su: subject, and so on. The computer searches the fields to retrieve relevant records based on the words entered in a search string. Each record is a bibliographic description of a work; multiple such records make up a database. Records contain information that allows the identification of a specific work. Records also describe the citation and can also include abstracts or full text documents.

AUTHOR   Holloran, Peter C., 1947-

TITLE   Boston's wayward children : social services for homeless children, 1830-1930 / Peter C. Holloran.

PUBLISHER   Rutherford [N.J.] : Fairleigh Dickinson ; London ; Cranbury, NJ : Associated University Presses, c1989.

SUBJECT   Children -- Institutional care -- Massachusetts -- Boston -- History.
Social work with children -- Massachusetts -- Boston -- History.
Abandoned children -- Services for -- Massachusetts -- Boston -- History.
Child welfare -- Massachusetts -- Boston -- History.

LOCATION	CALL NO.	STATUS
1 > ZIM	HV885 B7 H65 1989	CHECK SHELVES

Fig. 5.1

Knowing the content of the database is important when conducting a search. Databases may be specific to a particular discipline or subject, broad or narrow in coverage, offer access to a number of material types, and contain various dates of coverage. Relevant questions, including the following, need to be asked when deciding on an appropriate database to search:

1. What is the content and description of the database?

2. What types of materials are indexed in the database?

3. What is the time coverage of the database?

4. When was the database last updated? And how often is it updated?

5. What fields are searchable?

6. Is there a printed resource for this database for retrospective research?

Each database may differ in terms of content, coverage, and software commands, but the basic conceptual structure of fields, records, and multiple records making up a database will remain the same.

Vocabulary

Words are the heart of research. Words allow us to communicate with each other and define our ideas. All research must begin with words. As researchers begin to identify words and vocabulary that are relevant to the topic, they need to know the appropriate terms used within each specific database to effect the search. Many times a researcher inputs terms in a database and comes up with no relevant records. The negative search results do not necessarily mean that the database does not have information on the topic but, rather, that the researcher is not using the appropriate terminology. As researchers switch from one database to another, the vocabulary may also have to be changed. Brainstorming for vocabulary is a good way to begin creating a list of relevant terms and synonyms on a topic.

Free text, natural language, and word searches allow the researcher to search without knowing a specific vocabulary. Most databases and on-line catalogs allow word searches on a variety of fields. When a word search is executed, the computer may search multiple fields within each record such as the title, abstract, descriptor, or subject fields. If a researcher is unfamiliar with a controlled vocabulary, the word search may be a good place to start. The researcher can then identify the correct vocabulary used by the system in the subject or descriptor fields for a more accurate and specific search.

Databases with a controlled vocabulary have specific and fixed terminology. The databases may have an on-line thesaurus or a printed copy where the researcher can look up relevant terms. Terms may be listed as subject headings, descriptors, identifiers, or by topic. Some databases also have an on-line word index that identifies what words are used and how often they appear in the database. Most on-line catalogs use the Library of Congress Subject Headings (LCSH) as a controlled vocabulary. But many databases have their own thesaurus specific to the content or discipline of the materials indexed. Compiling a vocabulary list of similar and related terms results in multiple examples that may be helpful when searching different databases.

Boolean Logic

Boolean Logic Operators allow the researcher to narrow terms, broaden terms, and exclude terms. The operators are **AND**, **OR**, and **NOT**.

The Boolean Logic Operator **AND** is used to narrow searches. By using **AND,** the search will combine terms and concepts. As an example, two search concepts such as "health care **AND** homeless" could be combined. This search will result in the retrieval of records that contain health care and homeless. In some databases the **AND** is implied and does not need to be included in the search command. Other databases are case sensitive and require the **AND** to be capitalized; others will allow either upper or lower case. The **AND** will combine more than two concepts by entering multiple terms: "health care **AND** homeless **AND** Albuquerque."

The **OR** Boolean Logic Operator allows the searcher to expand search terms using synonyms for related terms. To expand a search on homeless, the searcher can combine possible related terms such as "homeless **OR** vagrant **OR** itinerant **OR** lacking housing." The search will result in the retrieval of all records that contain one or more of the terms.

Homeless **AND** health care

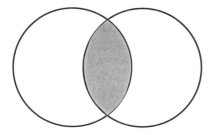

Fig. 5.2.

Homeless **OR** lacking housing

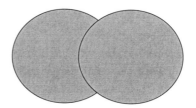

Fig. 5.3.

The **NOT** operator allows the researcher to exclude terms, narrowing a search. If a researcher wants to obtain information on the health care of homeless children, they can exclude terms such as elderly or senior citizens by using **NOT**. Use this command cautiously because of the possibility of excluding relevant information. For example, a document that includes the health care for both homeless children and elderly adults would be excluded.

Children **NOT** elderly

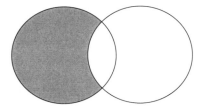

Fig. 5.4.

Another way to broaden the search is to use word truncation. Truncation allows the searcher to find root words or word suffixes. To search for homeless or homelessness, by using the truncation symbol, the searcher would retrieve both forms of the word by using homeless*. Databases differ by using a variety of commands for the truncation symbol, which might include *, +, ?, or !

Most databases have some form of Boolean Logical Operators imbedded within their software. Reading the help screens and identifying search commands before beginning a search will save time and help to execute an effective search.

EVALUATION OF INFORMATION

Not all information is equal in quality and accuracy. Nor is all information written without bias. As information is rapidly disseminated and accessed in today's electronic environment, it is necessary to apply critical thinking to the evaluation of that information. Identifying the differences between popular literature and scholarly literature is also important in the critical evaluation process. Professors often ask students to find scholarly articles, and tutors will need to explain to tutees how to distinguish between the two. Tutors must develop the skills needed to evaluate informational resources and materials based on five areas of criteria: accuracy, authority, objectivity, currency, and coverage. When selecting, reading, and assimilating information, the following questions need to be examined to determine the value of the information collected.

Accuracy of Information

- Has the information been verified by an editor?
- Are facts and statistics documented?
- Does the author provide citations to referenced works?

Authority of information

- Who is the author?
- What are the author's qualifications?
- Is the publisher reputable?
- Is the article peer reviewed?

Objectivity of Information

- Is the author's purpose clearly stated?
- Can biases be recognized?
- Can you distinguish between facts and opinions?

Currency of Information

- What is the copyright date?
- Have there been later editions or supplements?
- Are facts and statistics current?

Coverage of Information

- What topics are covered?
- Is the coverage an overview or in-depth?

This model of criteria provides a framework for tutors to follow. Enabling tutors and students to objectively assess the information they have gathered empowers them to become critical thinkers.

The five major concepts described in this chapter make up the basic curriculum for the library instruction tutor program. The following chapter introduces the training program and practical applications.

REFERENCES

Weil, Michelle M., and Larry D. Rosen. 1997. *TechnoStress*. New York: John Wiley.

ADDITIONAL READINGS

Aitchison, Jean, and Alan Gilchrist. 1987. *Thesaurus construction: A practical manual*. London: Aslib.

Barclay, Donald A., ed. *Teaching electronic information literacy: A-how-to-do-it manual*. 1995. New York: Neal-Schuman.

Chamis, Alice Yanosko. 1991. *Vocabulary control and search strategies in online searching*. New York: Greenwood Press.

Fink, Deborah. 1989. *Process and politics in research: A model for course design*. Chicago: American Library Association.

Immroth, John Phillip. 1971. *A guide to the Library of Congress classification*. Littleton, Colo.: Libraries Unlimited.

Lancaster, F. W. 1986. *Vocabulary Control for Information Retrieval*. Arlington, Va.: Information Resources Press.

MacDonald, Linda Brew, et al. 1990. *Teaching technologies in libraries: A practical guide*. Boston: G. K. Hall.

Slavens, Thomas P. 1994. *Reference interviews, questions, and materials*. 3rd ed. Metuchen, N.J.: Scarecrow Press.

Chapter 6

Library Instruction Tutor Training Program: Applications

In Chapter 5, we discussed the major concepts and curriculum of the LITP. In this chapter, we explain how to adapt those concepts into eight two-hour training sessions. The first hour is devoted to lecture and demonstration by the LITC and other library personnel. The second hour is for hands-on exercises or group activities for the library instruction tutors. Included in each session is a description of the objectives, outline guide or lesson plan, follow-up activities and practice, and a reading list to reinforce the concepts covered.

The session objectives serve several purposes. The first purpose is to identify and build specific library skills for application in an academic setting. The second is to incorporate these basic concepts into lifelong use of information, information sources, and information systems. The objectives also articulate what is expected of the library instruction tutors and create an understanding of what they are responsible for learning. The objectives also set boundaries for the library instruction tutors on what will be covered in a tutoring session.

The outline guide accompanying each session serves as a resource for the library instruction tutors while they are participating in a tutoring session. These guides are designed to help the tutors remember what they have learned once they begin to tutor.

The follow-up, hands-on activities help to reinforce what was taught in the tutoring session and also assist the tutors in learning the information on their own. Activities include individual tours, worksheets, and practice exercises. In the second hour of training, the tutors begin each activity with the LITC present and then continue to work on their own until the next training session. At the beginning of each training session, a review of the previous session is conducted and time for questions and answers is allotted.

The Rainbow Book readings serve as a companion reference for each individual library instruction tutor. It can be a compilation of library information guides, session objectives, outline guides, articles, handouts, and maps that the library instruction tutors can refer to and read. The Rainbow Book assignments are given as outside reading and can be read on the job while the library instruction tutors are not with a tutee.

The following eight sessions can be used as a model for a Library Instruction Tutoring Training Program. The sessions can be modified to fit the information resources at individual libraries.

SESSION 1:
INTRODUCTION TO CAMPUS LIBRARIES

The library instruction tutors are responsible for knowing the physical layout and services provided by each library on campus. This allows them to make proper referrals, provide directions, and understand the library arrangement.

Tour of Libraries: The tutors begin by taking a tour of the main or undergraduate library on campus. To familiarize themselves with the physical layout and facilities of the library, they need to locate and identify the following areas: book stacks, periodicals, microforms, electronic resources, indexes and abstracts, on-line and card catalog, telephones, rest rooms, and study rooms.

Library Services: The tour also includes the library services available to students. This part of the tour covers what services are offered at reference, circulation, reserves, interlibrary loan, special collections, government information, copy services, personnel, and special collections.

Library Arrangement: The tutors also need to understand how the library is arranged by LC call numbers and other call number systems as appropriate. If there are branch libraries at the institution, they need to know what sections of the LC are housed at each branch. Most libraries have a call number location chart that shows the breakdown. Books, periodicals, and microforms are sometimes housed in different locations, and an explanation for this should be given. This part of the orientation is necessary because tutors will be responsible for providing informal tours to students.

Outline Guide for a Tour of an
Undergraduate Library

Objectives

The library instruction tutors will:

- Understand library policies and procedures
- Understand the way collections and services are physically organized and accessed
- Understand the inter-relatedness of library departments, sections, and units
- Understand the libraries' grouping of information by subject, author, format, and special audiences.

I. Tour Reference and Information

The reference staff provides information on library resources, services, and facilities. Reference personnel are there to answer questions, and students should be encouraged to ask them. Appointments can also be made for in-depth research consultations.

II. Tour Reference Collection

Reference materials include dictionaries, encyclopedias, almanacs, handbooks, biographical directories, bibliographies, and many other works. The collection may also contain indexes to periodical literature in hard copy and electronic format.

III. Tour On-line and Card Catalog

In the reference area and other areas of the library, students may be able to access the on-line catalog. Tutors will need to distinguish between the on-line catalog and other computerized work areas. Some libraries may also have card catalogs still in use and on-line and card catalogs should be consulted for comprehensive research.

IV. Interlibrary Loan

Materials not available on campus can be borrowed from other libraries. Requests for books and articles from other libraries can be made through Interlibrary Loan.

V. Computerized Research Area

Reference departments have various computerized systems that access indexes, abstracts, CD-ROMs, and the Internet. Each computer workstation is labeled for specific databases and may have sign-up sheets.

VI. Circulation Desk

The Circulation Desk is where students can go to check out, recall, and put holds on books, periodicals, and government information. Tutors should be briefed on the circulation policies for loan periods and the identification necessary for obtaining a library card.

VII. Reserve Desk

Faculty members may place books and other materials "on reserve" for related course readings. The Reserve Desk checks materials out to students, and loan periods will differ from those of the Circulation Desk. The student will need to know the professor's name and course number to retrieve reserve items.

VIII. Government Information

The United States Government Printing Office publishes documents and materials covering many topics and disciplines. The University of New Mexico General Library (UNMGL) is a Regional Depository that retains and houses all information distributed by the U.S. government. Government information is classified by the SuDocs call number system. This system groups information according to the issuing agency.

IX. Special Collections

Special Collections consists of a special-care facility for archives, manuscripts, historical photographs, architectural documents, and rare books. The books, periodicals, microforms, manuscripts, and photographs are non-circulating, which means that they must be used in the Special Collections area.

X. Periodicals and Newspaper Areas

Microforms are printed items that have been greatly reduced in size and can be read with the assistance of specially designed machines. They include microfilm, microfiche, and microcard. Microforms may be magazines, journals, newspapers, or entire books.

XI. Book Stacks and Call Number Location Charts

Circulating books are located on the second and third floors. Call number location charts can be picked up in the Reference area. The chart explains what call numbers are located at each library and on what floor of the individual building.

XII. Library Administration and Personnel

The offices of the Dean of Library Services and the administrative support staff are located on the second floor. This office maintains the lost-and-found items, which may be claimed from 8 a.m. to 5 p.m., Monday through Friday. The library's employment office is located in Personnel.

XIII. Disabled Student Services

Assistance in locating materials and using library facilities is available to all library patrons with disabilities. The staff at the Circulation Desk will locate and retrieve materials for disabled library users. The Alice S. Clark room is also available and is specially equipped for use by individuals with disabilities.

Activities

1. After the tour, and after reading about the library, the tutors can do their own self-guided tour and/or give each other tours. This will enable them to become familiar with the building, services, and resources available. It will also build their confidence in having practiced giving a tour before actually showing a tutee around.

2. Visit to other libraries on campus. After having had a thorough tour of the main or undergraduate library, the tutors can begin to visit and become familiar with the other libraries on campus. Other libraries may include a science and engineering library, fine arts library, business library, heath sciences library, or law library. They can do this individually, or in a group. During each library visit, they should each draw a simple map identifying the following services in each library: circulation, reference areas, reserve desk, copy centers or photocopying areas, computerized searching, periodical/microform, book stacks, information handouts, interlibrary loan, rest rooms, study rooms, public telephones, and personnel offices.

Rainbow Book Readings

Library Handouts: Libraries on the Campus; Semester Hours; Self-Guided Library Tour; Government Information Department; Center for Southwest Research; Reference Department; Circulation Services; Library Services for Patrons with Disabilities; Interlibrary Loan Service; Copying Services; Document Delivery Service.

SESSION 2:
WINDOWS® 95 APPLICATIONS, INTERNET BROWSERS, AND COMPUTER ACCOUNTS

◀───▶

Library instruction tutors need to have a basic understanding of Windows applications to move easily through the available electronic systems. Although they are not responsible for tutoring Windows® applications, they do need to know the basic commands and functions. The tutors will be using a Web format for most of the tutoring sessions and must have a firm grounding in the use of browsers. Web browsers allow users to point and click with a mouse to navigate the Internet. The Netscape® browser is supported at UNM and is used as the Web browser example throughout all of the following sessions.

Library instruction tutors must also know how to access library resources from on or off campus. For referral purposes, they need to know where the computer pods or labs are located on campus and the hours of operation as well as locations within the library.

A computer account is a way to communicate and find informational resources at higher education institutions. Individual accounts enable students to send and receive electronic mail messages (e-mail), research the libraries' electronic resources, and access the Internet. Library instruction tutors will be responsible for teaching tutees how to send electronic bibliographic records to student e-mail accounts. When printing is unavailable, bibliographic records may be downloaded to a disk or an e-mail account. Library instruction tutors will also communicate with each other, and the LITC, through e-mail. Library systems and technology may change from one day to another, and e-mail messages provide an open communication resource to report and update those changes. The library instruction tutors are responsible for knowing how a student obtains a computer account and the account logon ID and password, as well as the appropriate uses of that account.

Outline Guide for Windows® 95, Netscape®, and Computer Accounts

Objectives

The library instruction tutors will:

- Understand the electronic information process
- Understand basic Windows® 95 applications
- Understand basic functions of browsers using Netscape®
- Understand policies, uses, and commands for e-mail.

I.   Introduction to Windows® 95

Demonstrate and practice basic Windows® 95 functions including: Program Manager, Menu bar, Control menu button, Toolbar, Minimize button, Maximize button, Close button, Folders, Files, Windows border, Status bar, Scroll bar, Icons, signing on and off the system.

II.   What is the Internet?

A.   Brief History

B.   What does it mean to "be on the Internet or the Web?"

1.   Electronic mail

2.   Telnet

3.   File Transfer Protocol

4.   World Wide Web

C.   World Wide Web

1.   The Web is a collection of standards and protocols used to access information available on the Internet. The Internet is the network used to transport information.

2.   Web Standards:

a.   URL (Uniform Resource Locator)

b.   HTTP (Hypertext Transfer Protocol)

c.   HTML (Hypertext Markup Language)

D.   Equipment and Connections

1.   Computer

2.   Communication modem

3.   Direct Internet connection

4.   Internet software

a.   SLIP or PPP

b.   TCP/IP software

c.   Browser (such as Netscape® or Explorer®)

III.   Introduction to Netscape® Browser

A.   UNM General Library Home Page (http://eLibrary.unm.edu/) Accessed May 30, 2000.

1.   Title bar (Name of Current Document)

2.   Navigational aids

a.   Highlighted words that link you to other multimedia pages

3.   Progress bar

a.   Status of retrieved document

    4. Address location field

       a. URL address of current document

  B. Graphical Interface Tools

    1. Hyperlinks: Click on highlighted words (colored and/or underlined) to bring another page of related information to your screen.

    2. Auto-Loaded Images

    3. Web images can be documents, photographs, movies, video, and/or sound.

  C. Linking via buttons and pull-down menus

    1. Demonstrate browser navigational button tools

       a. Back, Forward, Home, Reload, Images, Open, Print, Find, Stop

    2. Demonstrate browser navigational pull-down menus

       a. File, Go, Bookmarks, Directory, Options

IV. PINE e-mail system

  A. Demonstrate and practice the following e-mail functions: logging on and off system using name and password; Help; composing and sending messages; folders; address book setup; configure PINE options; and quit program.

Activities

1. Practice Windows® 95 On-line Tutorial

2. Tutors practice e-mailing messages to each other and friends during the training session to become familiar with the e-mail system.

3. Practice Exercises (See Appendix C).

Rainbow Book Readings

Raeder, Aggi. 1995. The Internet Express: Web Browsers for Searchers. *Searcher* 3 (9): 42–46.

Sterling, Bruce. 1993. Science: Internet. *Magazine of Fantasy and Science Fiction* 84 (2): 99–107.

Library Handouts: Creating an E-mail account, How to use PINE, Introduction to Netscape®.

SESSION 3:
INFORMATION CYCLE AND RESEARCH INSTRUCTION

Assisting students with library research instruction will be a large part of what the library instruction tutors will do. A good search strategy saves the tutor and the tutee time while they are learning to access the most useful information for the tutee's research project. Systematic ways of narrowing or broadening a topic guide the tutors and students to appropriate resources. Tutors may begin by identifying the research needed as primary or secondary, and then identifying the format of either books or periodicals.

Outline Guide for Search Instruction

Objectives

The library instruction tutors will:

- Understand library research instruction pathways

- Understand the concept of controlled vocabulary

- Understand library resources

- Understand library call number systems

- Construct an appropriate search strategy

- Understand the difference between the use of primary and secondary sources

- Understand how to refine or reformulate research topics based upon scope, direction, time frame, or other factors

- Understand the organization and communication of information within disciplines

- Identify when a question is interdisciplinary.

I.   Information Cycle

    A.   How information is created

        1.   Author/Communicator

        2.   Publisher

        3.   Distribution

        4.   Indexing

    B. How information is organized in libraries
   1. Acquired
   2. Catalog
   3. Classified
      a. LCSH
      b. Dewey Decimal
      c. SuDocs

    C. How information is accessed and retrieved
   1. Indexes
   2. Abstracts
   3. Catalogs

II. Research Strategies

    A. Select a topic
   1. Primary or Secondary Material needed
      a. Primary: Letters, diaries, speeches, interviews
      b. Secondary: Newspapers/periodicals indexes, books, government documents, encyclopedias

    B. Have you focused your topic? Use Search Strategies Worksheet (see Appendix C)
   1. Too broad? Limit by time period, geographic location, or population group
   2. Too narrow
   3. Too current

    C. Establish Vocabulary
   1. Brainstorm for synonyms and other ideas
   2. Subject thesauri
   3. LCSH

    D. Gathering Information
   1. Background Information
      a. Encyclopedias and dictionaries
      b. Reference sources
      c. Books
   2. Current Information
      a. Periodical and abstracting indexes/databases
      b. Newspaper indexes/databases
      c. World Wide Web

      3.   Additional Information
         a. Statistical sources
         b. Biographical sources
         c. Geographical sources
         d. Government information
         e. Bibliographies

E. References
    1. Librarians
    2. Professors
    3. Experts

Activities

1. Tutors can begin researching topics with each other through the use of role-playing and mock tutoring exercises.

2. Practice Exercises: Search Strategies Worksheet, LCSH, and controlled vocabulary. (See Appendix C.)

Rainbow Book Readings

Fink, Deborah. 1989. *Process and Politics in Library Research: A Model for Course Design*. Chicago: American Library Association. Chapters 2, 4, and 6.

    Library Handouts: Library Research Step By Step; Choosing a Topic to Research; Search Strategy; Boolean Logical Operators

SESSION 4:
INTRODUCTION TO THE LIBRARY CATALOG

◄──►

Library instruction tutors need to understand the basic concepts of library catalogs, on-line and card. A library catalog can be defined as a collection of local library holdings and/or other library holdings. The tutors may not know what "holdings" are because the term is part of library jargon and needs to be clarified. Holdings can be classified as books, journal titles, government publications, audiovisual material, sound recordings, musical scores, and special collections. Each unique holding has a bibliographic record that lists the title, author, subject, publisher, call number, and other important information about an individual item. These individual items make up the contents of the library catalog.

This session introduces the tutors to the three concepts of searching and applies them directly to the on-line catalog.

Outline Guide for the Library Catalog

Objectives

The library instruction tutors will:

- Understand the ways information is stored and retrieved
- Understand database structure of fields, bibliographic records, and databases
- Understand database content, date of coverage, limits, truncation, and help screens
- Understand Boolean logic operators
- Understand controlled, word, and phrase vocabulary searching
- Understand the content of bibliographic citations
- Find and locate material within the libraries' different collections
- Understand differing locations and library holdings
- Download, print, and e-mail citations.

I. LIBROS, the LIBRary On-line System

    A. Vocabulary

        1. LCSH

        2. Word Search

        3. Phrase Searching

B.   Boolean Logic
1.   AND
2.   OR
3.   NOT

C.   Database Structure
1.   Contents: books, periodicals/journals, government publica-
     tions, audiovisual material, sound recordings, musical scores,
     and special collections
2.   Searchable fields: word, subject, author, title, content notes,
     course reserves, call numbers, and standard numbers
3.   Date of Coverage
     a.   On-line Catalog: materials received after 1975
     b.   Card Catalog: materials received before 1975
4.   Limits
     a.   Truncation symbol *: truncates root words
     b.   Language, material type, publisher, year of publication,
          location of item, words in the author, title, or subject
     c.   Case sensitivity
5.   Interpretation of bibliographic citations
6.   Download, print, e-mail
7.   Retrieve physical documents from search
8.   Interlibrary loan

Activities

- Practice exercises (See Appendix C).

Rainbow Book Readings

Library Handouts: On-line Catalog: Finding Books, Periodicals, and
Government Information; Call Number Classification Systems; Location Codes
in the On-line Catalog; Call Number and Locations.

SESSION 5:
INTRODUCTION TO
EBSCOHOST ACADEMIC SEARCH FULLTEXT ELITE

As with the on-line catalog, the three concepts for searching can and should be applied to electronic periodical databases. *EBSCOhost's Academic Search FullTEXT Elite* is a multidisciplinary database that can be searched using the three concepts. Tutors will also be introduced to a new concept of natural language searching, which will be discussed further in the World Wide Web session. The session includes a lecture and database demonstration with an hour of hands-on practice.

Outline Guide to
EBSCOhost Academic Search FullTEXT Elite

Objectives

The library instruction tutors will:

- Understand the ways in which articles are stored and retrieved
- Understand database structure of fields, bibliographic records, and databases
- Understand database content, date of coverage, limits, and help screens
- Understand Boolean logic operators
- Understand keyword searching
- Understand natural language searching
- Understand the content of bibliographic records
- Retrieve journal titles and articles held in the library
- Download, print, and e-mail citations and full-text articles.

I. *EBSCOhost Academic Search FullTEXT Elite*

    A. Vocabulary

        1. Keyword

        2. Natural language

        3. Browse

B. Boolean Logic – AND, OR, NOT

    1. Basic search

    2. Advanced search

C. Database Structure

    1. Content: Multidisciplinary database that includes 3,200 journal titles with 1,000 full-text titles.

    2. Date of Coverage: Varies from title to title with some dating back to the early 1980s.

    3. Limits

        a. Truncation Symbol *, truncates root words

        b. Full text, journal title, date of publication, peer reviewed, illustrations

        c. Not case sensitive

    4. Interpretation of bibliographic citations

    5. Download, print, e-mail citations and full-text articles

    6. Retrieve physical articles

        a. LIBROS, on-line catalog

        b. Interlibrary Loan

Activities

1. On-line tutorial

2. Practice exercises (See Appendix C)

3. Accessing and retrieving information in various formats; that is, full-text on-line, microfilm, microfiche, and paper.

Rainbow Book Readings

Tomaiuolo, Nicholas G., and Joan Packer. 1998. Maximizing Relevant Retrieval. *Online* 22 (6): 57–60.

Library Handouts: Popular vs. Scholarly literature

SESSION 6:
INTRODUCTION TO FIRSTSEARCH®

The FirstSearch® system is composed of 60 on-line databases. Library instruction tutors search multidisciplinary and specific subject databases. Library instruction tutors will be responsible for assisting tutees in identifying databases that meet the tutees' research needs. Although the software is the same for each database, each database may have different vocabulary, limits, commands, and functions. The first hour of this session is dedicated to an overview of the system, with a demonstration followed up in the second hour with hands-on activities.

Outline Guide to FirstSearch®

Objectives

The library instruction tutors will:

- Understand when to use appropriate databases based on search topic

- Understand multidisciplinary and subject databases

- Understand database structures

- Understand database content, date of coverage, limits, truncation, help screens, and other unique features within databases

- Understand controlled, word, and phrase vocabularies

- Understand content of bibliographic citations

- Find and locate relevant material in campus libraries

- Process interlibrary loan requests

- Download, print, and e-mail citations.

I. FirstSearch® via Netscape®
    A. Vocabulary
        1. LCSH and modified LCSH
        2. Subject thesauri
        3. Word searching
        4. Phrase searching

B. Boolean Logic – AND, OR, NOT

    1. Basic Search

    2. Advanced Search

C. Database Structure – Unique to each of the 60 databases

    1. Content and database description

    2. Dates of coverage

    3. Limits

    4. Interpretation of bibliographic citations

    5. Download, print, e-mail

    6. Retrieve documents from search using full text, LIBROS, or interlibrary loan.

Activities

1. FirstSearch® On-line tutorial

2. Practice exercises (See Appendix C)

Rainbow Book Readings

Library Handout: UNM FirstSearch®.

SESSION 7:
INTRODUCTION TO THE WORLD WIDE WEB

The library instruction tutors have been using the Web in all the other electronic sessions and should be comfortable using Netscape® by now. The tutors are responsible for explaining the Web to tutees. The Web incorporates some common features of database searching but also has several unique features. The tutors will practice and learn about Yahoo!®, a directory search engine; AltaVista®, a keyword search engine; and Northern Light®, a multiple database search engine. They will conduct their searches from the UNM site http://elibrary.umn.edu/libinfo/Search/internet.html (accessed May 30, 2000). This site has documentation on the introduction of search engines and direct links to the search engines. The first hour is limited to a brief lecture and on-line demonstration of the various search engines, and the second hour is devoted to hands-on practice for the tutors.

Outline Guide for the World Wide Web

Objectives

The library instruction tutors will:

- Understand the similarities and differences in search engines

- Understand controlled, word, and phrase searching

- Understand the structure of Web pages, fields, summaries, and full text

- Understand search engine content, date of coverage limits, truncation, and help screens

- Understand basic and advanced search screens and apply Boolean logic

- Understand relevancy ranking in search engines

- Download, print, and e-mail.

I. World Wide Web (http://elibrary.umn.edu/libinfo/Search/internet.html) Accessed June 1, 2000.

    A. Search Engines: Descriptions and definitions

        1. Keyword search engines

        2. Subject/Directory search engines

        3. Multiple or meta search engines

B. Vocabulary
   1. Word searching
   2. Phrase searching

C. Boolean logic – AND, OR, NOT, AND NOT, or BUT NOT
   1. Basic search screens
   2. Advanced search screens

D. Relevancy Ranking
   1. Frequency of terms
   2. Proximity of terms
   3. Ranking of documents

E. Database Structure
   1. Searchable fields, that is titles, summary, URLs, meta tags, etc.
   2. Web page – definition and description
   3. Dates of coverage
   4. Limits
      a. Truncation
      b. Language, date, and illustrations
      c. Case sensitivity
   5. Interpretation of Web page citation
   6. Download, print, e-mail

Activities

1. Practice exercises (See Appendix C)

Rainbow Book Readings

Ardito, Stephanie C. 1998. The Internet: Beginning or End of Organized Information *Searcher* 6 (1): 52–57.

Cram, Carol M. 1997. *World Wide Web: Illustrated Projects*. North Vancouver, B.C.: Course Technology.

Kohnen, Carol. 1998. A Brief History of the Internet and the World Wide Web. *Missouri Library World* 3 (2): 1.

Lester, Dan. 1995. Yahoo! Profile of a Web Database. *Database* 18 (6): 46–50.

Minkel, Walter. 1997. Lost (& Found) in Cyberspace. *School Library Journal* 43 (3): 102–105.

SESSION 8:
EVALUATION OF INFORMATION

$$\longleftrightarrow$$

Library instruction tutors will be helping tutees find relevant research on a specific topic. Library instruction tutors need to understand how to interpret relevant information and research. They will question tutees while searching databases on relevant citations. By applying the critical evaluation of information and practicing the analysis of information, library instruction tutors will be equipped to assist tutees in finding appropriate resources.

Outline Guide:
Introduction to the Evaluation of Information and Scholarly and Popular Literature

Objectives

The library instruction tutors will:

- Understand the criteria for evaluating information
- Understand the criteria for popular literature
- Understand the criteria for scholarly literature
- Identify relevant citations.

I.   Critical Evaluation of Information
    A.   Accuracy of Information
        1.   Has the information been verified by an editor?
        2.   Are facts and statistics documented?
        3.   Does the author provide citations to referenced works?
    B.   Authority of Information
        1.   Who is the author?
        2.   What are the author's qualifications?
        3.   Is the publisher reputable?
        4.   Is the article peer reviewed?
    C.   Objectivity of Information
        1.   Is the author's purpose clearly stated?
        2.   Can biases be recognized?
        3.   Can you distinguish between facts and opinions?

    D. Currency of Information

       1. What is the copyright date?

       2. Have there been later editions or supplements?

       3. Are the facts and statistics current?

    E. Coverage of Information

       1. What topics are covered?

       2. Is the coverage an overview or in-depth?

II.   Popular versus Scholarly Literature Guideline Criteria

    A. Purpose

       1. Popular: Articles inform or entertain.

       2. Scholarly: Articles present news and results of original research from scholars and professionals.

    B. Audience

       1. Popular: General population and mass audience.

       2. Scholarly: Specialized interest group such as scholars and professionals.

    C. Appearance

       1. Popular: Covers are colorful and attractive.

       2. Scholarly: Covers usually only have one or two colors and have a basic graphic design.

    D. Style

       1. Popular: Articles are written at a low reading level and do not contain technical language.

       2. Scholarly: Articles are serious and use specialized or technical language.

    E. Authors

       1. Popular: Editorial staff members or freelance writers.

       2. Scholarly: Scholars or professional in a specific field. Write to communicate with colleagues.

    F. Publisher

       1. Popular: Commercially published. Articles tend to be reports or opinion pieces based upon the research of others.

       2. Scholarly: Published by an association or academic institution. Articles are subject to the peer review process and are based on research.

G. Advertising

    1. Popular: Advertise a wide variety of products and services.

    2. Scholarly: Few or no advertisements.

H. Citations

    1. Popular: Rarely include full citations of sources.

    2. Scholarly: Sources are always cited through footnotes, endnotes or bibliographies.

Activities

1. Tutors are given two articles, one from a popular magazine and one from a scholarly journal covering the same subject. They use the above criteria and compare and contrast the differences between the two articles.

2. Tutors search periodical databases and, using the above criteria, evaluate articles on a topic of their own. They also analyze relevant information using the critical evaluation criteria.

Rainbow Book Readings

Fink, Deborah. 1989. *Process and Politics in Library Research: A Model for Course Design*. Chicago: American Library Association. Chapter 10, Critical Evaluation.

West, Charles K. 1981. *The Social and Psychological Distortion of Information*. Chicago: Nelson-Hall. Chapters 1–7.

Library Handouts: Magazines and Journals: A Comparison.

Once the initial Library Instruction Tutor Training Program has been completed, on-going training by the LITC can be accomplished at library instruction tutor team and individual meetings and through e-mail. The assigned activities and readings help to reinforce the concepts and to engage the library instruction tutors in practicing the learned skills. The concepts and skills that library instruction tutors learned during the training sessions can also be transferred to other databases. The library instruction tutors can now apply those skills toward learning ProQuest®, Lexis-Nexis®, UnCover®, Statistical Universe®, and other databases available at the local institution. The LITC will continue to be available for the library instruction tutees to ask questions regarding the library instruction tutoring content.

The following chapter serves as a model of how to "pull it all together." In Chapter 7, we explain how the LITP was planned, created, implemented, and evaluated. We also explain institutional anecdotes and changes made along the way within the collaborative program. We hope that it serves as a successful model for a Library Instruction Tutoring Program.

University of New Mexico General Library Experience

In 1995, the Library Instruction Tutor Program was not a new idea at UNM. The idea had been proposed many times but it did not come to fruition until the library administration, faculty, and staff made a commitment with the Center for Academic Program Support (CAPS), the campus learning center. Members of CAPS originally proposed the idea of Library Instruction Tutors. The CAPS staff and tutors noted that tutees asked for help with research during discipline-specific tutoring sessions. The writing lab tutors were often asked to help find articles or books for the tutees. When writing lab tutors would suggest that a student writing a research paper use LIBROS, the on-line catalog, the tutees often would respond, "What's LIBROS?" The writing lab tutors would help as much as time allowed, but their main focus was to tutor writing skills. These observations led to the recognition of the need for and conception of a Library Instruction Tutoring Program.

PROGRAM STRUCTURE

Having the learning center located within the undergraduate library is unique to UNM's General Libraries (GL). CAPS has been a department within the library since 1980. The Library and CAPS worked together to provide support and assistance to students. It seemed natural to develop and institute a Library Instruction Tutoring Program because of the similar philosophies and goals in higher education between both organizations. This chapter describes the planning, implementation, and evaluation of the UNM LITP Pilot Project during 1995–1996 and the continuation of the LITP thereafter.

The collaborative effort began in the fall of 1995 when the General Library assigned a Faculty Librarian as the Library Instruction Tutor Coordinator (LITC). The LITCs duties included creating a Library Instruction Tutor Training Curriculum and serving as the LI Team Leader during the fall of

1996. (See Appendix B for Team Leader Duties.) As part of the collaboration, the LITC also participated in all CAPS training sessions in the fall of 1995 and winter of 1996. This allowed the LITC to become familiar with the learning center's policies, procedures, and the daily responsibilities of the tutors.

During the pilot project phase it was decided that the LITP would be housed and based within CAPS. Library instruction tutors would use the one-on-one tutoring model for all tutoring appointments during the project phase as well. UNM undergraduate and graduate students were eligible to use library instruction tutoring services. CAPS allowed 100 minutes of tutoring for each course or subject area per week in 25- or 50-minute time blocks. Tutees could make appointments to see a tutor one week in advance, either by phone or in person. The library instruction tutors would begin taking one-on-one appointments during the third week of classes in the fall of 1996. The first two weeks of classes were devoted to library instruction tutor training.

PLANNING

Once the LITC had been identified, implementation dates were set and the real planning was in process. The curriculum content and design was to be completed within the academic year 1995–1996. Needs assessments, student input surveys, and analysis of data also needed to be completed by the end of the spring semester of 1996. Implementation of the LITP pilot project was scheduled for the fall of 1996.

Needs Assessment

The first step in determining the curriculum was to define our target audience for this service. Through collaborative efforts, the library instruction pilot project would target the new users of the library and the lower level undergraduates, but not be restricted to that group exclusively. One of the goals was to make students familiar with library services, resources, and research strategies. The tutoring sessions would not replace reference services but better prepare the students to request information and use electronic resources. The tutors would help students with fundamentals of research and library orientation.

For more information on the needs assessment, the library instruction session evaluations were analyzed to determine a potential need for a LITP. Student comments on the evaluations mentioned the following: the library instructor went too fast; the student was lost after the first fifteen minutes of the demonstration; the student had questions and was too intimidated to ask; the student did not have enough time to practice; and the student wanted more individualized attention. All of these comments demonstrated a need for a LITP.

Reference personnel also observed and commented that students were requesting more individualized attention at the reference desk with the advent of new technologies and resources. Students' reference questions often turned into in-depth instruction sessions on how to use electronic search tools. The needs analysis identified several areas where a LITP would be useful and reconfirmed the commitment to implementing the program.

Student Input Survey

Direct input and opinions from UNM students helped establish the LITP curriculum and more clearly define a target audience. In order to obtain information from potential users of the LITP, we conducted a survey in the spring of 1996 at CAPS. The voluntary survey was handed out by tutors in all disciplines over a two-week period. A total of 91 forms were collected. (See Appendix B for the survey.) Sixty-six percent of the respondents said working with a Library Instruction Tutor would have helped them in the past year. Seventy-six percent of the respondents said they would be "somewhat likely" or "very likely" to sign up for a session with a LI Tutor. Additional written comments from students included the following:

> "This service would save me time."

> "I am not familiar with the library but would love to learn what resources are available and how to utilize them . . . especially the Internet."

> "I entered a search in LIBROS and found there was nothing there, but I know there is. A tutor could help me discover what I'm doing wrong."

The survey showed the need for an LI tutor program at UNM, identified a group of potential users, and also influenced the development of the LITP curriculum content.

Curriculum Input Survey

In most peer tutoring areas, a professor develops the curriculum and provides course content to students. Tutors for those courses gain their content skills by taking the course or a number of discipline-related courses. CAPS then provides training in how to be a tutor. The team leaders, graduate students in the content area, provide on-going discussion of content. Tutors offer assistance by helping students to process, understand, and retain the course content. This is the same course content that the tutors learned when they were enrolled in the course. With LI Tutors, the LITC faced the challenge of developing a curriculum that would be covered during the library instruction tutoring sessions.

During the fall 1995 semester, the LITC visited 12 departments within UNMGL and met with each public and technical service area to discuss curriculum development with faculty, staff, and student employees. Each meeting began with the question, "What library skills and strategies does the 'Introductory Student' need to be a successful researcher at the University of New Mexico General Library?" Brainstorming techniques were used to solicit ideas and suggestions. Copious notes were taken and all comments were considered. Sample curriculum suggestions included teaching the LI Tutor how to find and locate books and journal articles, how to understand the difference between a word search and a subject search, how to find reserve material, how to understand location codes for the different libraries on campus, and how to critically evaluate information.

During the spring of 1996, the suggestions and comments were analyzed for several main concepts and overlapping themes that created the curriculum. The overriding concept was one of "patterns." UNMGL faculty, staff, and students were unanimous in suggesting that the skills and strategies acquired from a library instruction tutor be transferable and applicable to all libraries. After analyzing the collected data, the following concepts emerged and became the Library Instruction Tutor Training Curriculum: Library Services and Policies; Search Strategies; Boolean Logic, Search Logic, and Limits; Vocabulary (Controlled vs. Word); and Database Structures.

IMPLEMENTATION OF THE PILOT PROGRAM

Considerations for the library instruction pilot project's implementation included discussions of clearly defined duties and responsibilities between the Library and CAPS. Discussions and decisions included identification of human resources, including the training of LI Tutors, and the operational needs, goals, and evaluations of the pilot project. The use of a collaborative model allowed CAPS and the Library to benefit from each other's strengths and expertise.

CAPS' responsibilities included recruiting, hiring, training, and evaluating the library instruction tutors. The LITC and other Library personnel were responsible for the content, evaluation, and on-going training of the Library Instruction Tutor Curriculum. New LI Tutors went through two areas of training. The first training curriculum was "how to be a tutor." LI Tutors were trained with other new tutors who had discipline specific areas. Tutor training was conducted by CAPS staff and was held the week before classes began in the fall of 1996. The LITC participated in all of the training with the new LI tutors.

The second half of the training was the Library Instruction Tutor Training curriculum content. The LITC and other library personnel conducted the training in the first two weeks of classes. The LI Tutors began tutoring one-on-one appointments in the third week of classes.

Human Resources

Recruiting and Hiring Library Instruction Tutors

Recruiting for LI Tutors began in April and May of 1996 and continued through the summer semester. The number of LI Tutors to hire was determined by the trends and hours observed by CAPS personnel. During the first semester we hired four students after evaluating the scalability of the program. Analysis of scalability was determined by several factors. One factor was that CAPS was open approximately 65 hours per week, so we tried to cover all available time with at least one LI Tutor.

When determining how many LI Tutors to hire, the CAPS management staff also looked for potential and current trends effecting enrollment at UNM. The first factor was the expected enrollment of new freshmen and returning students. The introduction of Lottery Bridge Scholarships, a program where New Mexico high school graduates come to UNM and receive free tuition, would increase UNM's freshmen class enrollment by 20 percent. This increase in students would bring an anticipated 20 percent increase in the use of CAPS and for LI Tutors as well. CAPS management also looked at curriculum changes. When the English 102 or Psychology 106 courses required research papers, the tutoring center would see an increase in usage, thus creating a potential higher demand for LI Tutors.

Work-study qualified students were preferred but not required. The tutoring services at CAPS were open Monday–Thursday from 9:00 a.m. to 7 p.m., Friday from 9:00 a.m. to 2 p.m., and Saturdays 11:00 a.m. to 4:00 p.m. Job advertisements were placed in the campus newspaper, *The Daily Lobo.*

During spring semester, the LITC visited five UNMGL Library Credit Courses, four Library Science Classes, and contacted students from previous Library Credit courses through e-mail. In each class, the LITC gave a brief presentation, described the new program, job duties and responsibilities, pay, and working environment. All interested students were encouraged to apply.

A willingness to learn, maturity, and a sense of responsibility were the most important prerequisites. The required qualities for a LI Tutor were a cumulative grade point average of 3.0 or higher, along with excellent communication, organization, and interpersonal skills, including the ability to listen and reflect back user concerns. Preferred qualities included a background in computers, prior tutoring experience, and demonstrated research skills. LI Tutors did not need to have a computer science background but minimal skills in computer applications and hardware and software would be beneficial. To better serve the university community, we actively recruited from all academic areas.

Each LI Tutor applicant was interviewed by the LITC and the CAPS Program Coordinator during the spring and summer semesters. The interviews lasted approximately one hour and included a description of the new program, duties and responsibilities, interview questions, and time for the candidate's questions. (See Appendix B for sample interview questions.) Applicants came from a variety of disciplines. Some candidates had specifically requested an application for a Library Instruction position whereas others were recruited from other subject tutoring specialties. From the pool of applicants, we also looked for a potential graduate student to fill the Library Instruction Tutor Team Leader position for the spring of 1997. The fall 1996 Team Leader position was filled by the LITC, who coordinated the curriculum and training program but turned over the specific duties of a team leader to a graduate student at the end of that semester.

During the first semester that CAPS implemented the LI Tutor pilot project, four tutors were hired. LI Tutor majors included a graduate student in Communication and Journalism, along with undergraduates in Linguistics, Anthropology, and Classical Guitar. All LI Tutors hired had met or exceeded the job requirements and prerequisites.

Center for Academic Program Support Training Responsibilities

CAPS was responsible for the training of LI Tutors in "how to be a tutor." The LI Tutors participated along side other new tutors during the training program.

In the fall of 1996, the hired LI Tutors began their training as New Tutors. The LITC also took part in the CAPS training as the current Library Instruction Team Leader. (See Appendix B for Team Leader Duties.) The CAPS tutor training program took place the week before classes started and before CAPS opened for business.

CAPS provided a two and a half-day training schedule for New, Regular, Advanced, and Master Tutor Training. For the purpose of this program only the New Tutor Training will be discussed. (See Appendix B for New Tutor Training Agenda.) New Tutor Training was for the newly hired tutors who had never tutored before and had to go through the basic level of training and complete 25 hours of tutoring before advancement to a Regular tutor. The training began with an introduction by the Director of CAPS, and was followed by a tour of CAPS facility and work area.

The Program Manager conducted an overview of the CAPS organization that covered specific information regarding the day-to-day workings of CAPS. Topics the Program Manager presented were standard services, description of the tutoring levels and requirements to meet those levels, tutor guidelines, work absences, schedules, payroll procedures, registration cards, and other essential information necessary to help the tutors be successful.

The tutors were also given an overview of the tutoring process. This included the philosophy of tutoring, ethics, boundaries, student-centered behavior, and principles and strategies. Advanced and Master Tutors assisted with the training by conducting mock tutoring sessions, and allowed the new tutors to critique and observe specific tutoring techniques. The Advanced and

Master Tutors also provided tips and suggestions that might be helpful to new tutors based on experiences that have worked for them.

The Learning Support Services staff educates New Tutors about students with learning disabilities. Tutors are given characteristics and definitions of students who may have difficulty with auditory processing, oral language, reading, writing, mathematics, organizational, and study or social skills, as well as guidelines and tutoring strategies to follow if they encounter a student with learning disabilities. Knowing how to provide a confidential and proper referral to Learning Support Services is a responsibility of the tutors.

The last section of New Tutor training covered the expected standards that tutors should abide by and a detailed description of the evaluation process. Tutors are formally evaluated twice a semester. They give evaluation forms to the tutees and ask them to complete the form at the end of the tutoring session. The evaluation form can also be used throughout the semester by tutees at any time. The evaluation process is an opportunity to recognize that the tutors are doing a good job. The tutors meet with the Team Leader to review the results once the information has been compiled. It also identifies areas that need improvement. (See Appendix B for a sample evaluation form.)

After the CAPS tutor training was completed, the LI Tutors began their training in the content area. The LITC and other Library personnel taught the Library Instruction Tutoring Training Curriculum.

Library Instruction Tutor Coordinator Training Responsibilities

The primary responsibility for the LITC during the 1995–1996 academic year was to develop the Library Instruction Tutor Training curriculum that would be implemented in the fall semester of 1996 during the pilot project. The LITC was also charged with providing leadership as the Library Instruction Team Leader during the pilot project. The LITC was responsible for providing instruction to the tutors on updates of changing information resources and technologies throughout the semester and following semesters.

The tutors had been trained on how-to-be a tutor before classes started and continued their library content training during the first and second week of classes. (See Appendix B for Library Instruction Tutor Training Agenda.) The content was covered in eight separate intensive two-hour training sessions. (See Chapter 6.) Each session devoted one hour to lecture and demonstration by the LITC and the second hour provided hands-on instruction and practice for the LI tutors. The sessions took place in a computer lab within the library that allowed each tutor to practice on individual PCs during the application and exercise portion. Library skills and strategies were reinforced by practice lessons that could be done outside of the training time. A schedule was devised for the two weeks of training when the LITC could meet with the newly hired LI Tutors. At the end of the two-week training schedule, the LI Tutors began taking one-on-one appointments.

Tutor Duties and Responsibilities

LI Tutors are expected to know the content area and also know tutoring strategies. During tutor training the LI Tutors are responsible for understanding and incorporating the following criteria into a tutoring session: be friendly and demonstrate an eagerness to help; be on time; be prepared; work scheduled hours; be receptive to questions; know the material covered; use examples to help students understand; prepare students to work independently; let students do most of the work; help students to understand general concepts as well as specific details; be patient and wait for student answers; monitor the balance of tutor–tutee talk; ask/use questions to direct students toward identifying what they know and need to know; and help students to summarize what they have learned during tutoring sessions. A sample case study LI tutor–tutee interaction that incorporates some of the above responsibilities is described in the following tutorial scenario. (See Appendix C for other sample tutoring scenarios.)

Case Study—The tutee is a returning student majoring in nursing. She is a wife and mother of two young children. She lives on a ranch 20 miles from Albuquerque and commutes to school during the day. Her experience with computers is limited. She has word processing experience but is unfamiliar with on-line searching and research skills. Her professor has assigned the class to write a paper including referenced citations from books or articles. She came to the library over the weekend and left frustrated because she did not have the proper research skills. She has signed up to meet with a LI Tutor and is ready for her 50-minute one-on-one appointment.

The LI Tutor greets the tutee in the waiting area, introduces himself, and leads the tutee to the tutoring area. Because this is the first time the tutee has been to CAPS the tutor has the tutee fill out a registration card and goes over the policies and rules with the tutee. (See Appendix B.) The tutor then has the tutee fill out the CAPS Library Instruction User Survey. After finishing the survey, the tutor quickly assesses that the tutee has little experience in performing library research. The tutee has not used the UNM library successfully and is unfamiliar with the on-line databases and search logic. She has used a library before but not a large academic library. As they discuss the tutee's research experience the tutor realizes that the session should start with the basics.

The tutor has the tutee sit at the computer and begins with the Search Strategy Worksheet. (See Appendix C.) This introduces the tutee to the concepts of vocabulary, Boolean logic, and record structure. It also helps to narrow her topic. The tutor has the tutee go to the UNM General Library Homepage and goes over what databases are accessible. Because the tutee needs to find background material and books, she selects and begins to search LIBROS, the on-line catalog. As they go through various searches the tutor asks the tutee questions that emphasize the details of the search. Questions include: What vocabulary terms are we searching for? What type of material is in this database? What is the call number for the book? Where is the book located? Who is the author? What other subject headings are used for this subject? What fields are being searched by the computer when entering a Word search? The tutee is at the computer and is executing all of the searches during the session.

After the tutee has found several useful citations the tutor assists the tutee in finding the material on the shelf in the library and explains the Library of Congress classification scheme. They then return to the tutoring area and within the remaining minutes the tutor queries the tutee to review what she has learned. The tutor also gives the tutee any Library handouts that might be helpful in searching the databases or understanding the concepts. Because the time is now over, the tutor suggests that the tutee sign up for other sessions. The tutee can be assisted with finding articles on her topic with the help of an LI Tutor. The tutee leaves the session empowered by new skills and feels comfortable searching the on-line catalog. The tutee makes another appointment to see an LI Tutor at a convenient time. After the tutee has gone, the LI Tutor writes a brief description of what was tutored on the back of the registration card. It is then filed so that the next time the student comes in, either he, or another tutor, will have a record of what was covered during the session. (See Appendix C for examples of Library Instruction Tutorial case studies.)

Operational Needs

Work Space and Materials

When the Library Instruction program began in the fall of 1996 the LI Tutors were using two 286 PC workstations, which were connected via the Ethernet to the computing center. Because of space limitations, the computer workstations were placed in a high-traffic public area. There were advantages and disadvantages to this location. One advantage was that the LI tutors were in a highly visible area and could be seen assisting students with library research needs. This visibility helped to publicize the new program and encouraged students to sign up for LI tutoring sessions.

The major disadvantage was the lack of privacy during tutoring sessions. LI Tutors felt they were on display. Another disadvantage was that the computer terminals were located in a public area where students were accustomed to using terminals for their own research needs. If a tutor needed one of the terminals for an appointment and it was in use, tutors would have to ask the student to leave that created several uncomfortable situations. It would also delay the actual tutoring session by five to ten minutes, making a 25-minute session only 15 minutes long.

The two 286 PCs were sufficient to begin the program in the fall of 1996 because most databases were accessed through a Telnet connection. But it soon became clear that two PCs were not enough. Only two tutors could be scheduled at the same time, and during peak tutoring hours, students were turned away because of a lack of equipment. Also during 1996, library technology and resources were changing from a Telnet connection to the Web environment. In 1997, the UNMGL Development Officer wrote a grant to obtain funds for the LITP. A $20,000 grant was awarded from the New Mexico Public Utilities Company. This donation allowed a classroom to be renovated into a computer workstation lab with more privacy for tutors and tutees. It also eliminated public access use, making the computers always available for tutoring sessions. We purchased six Pentium processors with 32 MB RAM and 15-inch monitors. The software installed included Windows®, the Netscape® graphical browser, Microsoft Word®, and the Mirada® suite. The tutors were then trained on a Windows® environment, and the electronic resources were updated to Web access capabilities.

The LI Tutors also need to have access to materials that would assist them during the tutoring sessions, so a small library of reference resource materials was started. It included dictionaries, subject thesauri, LCSH volumes, and library handouts. Each tutor was responsible for their own copy of the Rainbow Book, which included library exercises, readings, database descriptions, and other relevant material. (See Appendix C for Rainbow Book Table of Contents.)

Publicity

We took a cautious approach in publicizing the new LITP during the first semester. Card stock "tents" were made and displayed on the top of all computer terminals located in the reference areas of the Library (see Appendix B for a sample), which was an unobtrusive way to promote the program. The tents described the program and listed the hours that LI Tutors were available.

During the first month the LI Tutors needed to become familiar and feel comfortable with the content and with tutoring strategies. The CAPS administration encouraged all CAPS tutors who needed assistance with research sign up with an LI Tutor during work time. This helped the LI Tutors and other tutors who worked at CAPS become familiar with on-line databases and resources. Tutors were allowed to sign up during work time if they did not have a pending appointment. Word-of-mouth publicity quickly spread and the LI Tutors were seeing an increase in the number of tutees within the second, third, and fourth months of the program.

EVALUATION OF THE PILOT PROJECT AND FUTURE PLANS

Evaluation of the pilot project provided valuable information regarding the users of the program, the effectiveness of the LI Tutors, and allowed for feedback from library instruction tutors and others for future full implementation of the program.

Library Instruction User Survey

Assessing the users of the program was foremost in our evaluation. Knowing who used the services and their previous library instruction patterns would help to identify a target audience for the service. At the beginning of each tutorial session the LI Tutors had the tutees fill out the CAPS Library Instruction User Survey. (See Appendix B.) This survey provided the LI Tutor with an overview of the tutees research use and abilities and allowed the tutor to quickly assess the tutee's level of experience with research techniques. A profile of the tutees who participated in the Library Instruction Tutor pilot project provided valuable information about who the users were. Fifty percent of tutees had used a library one to three times a month. Twenty-two percent of tutees had never used a library before coming to UNM. The most used library resources by tutees included using the on-line catalog, the copy center, the reserve desk, and circulation services. Seventy-seven percent of the tutees had not attended a library instruction workshop; 70 percent of tutees could not explain Boolean operators, but 77 percent had requested assistance from the reference desk. Tutees' previous library training, before coming to UNM, included instruction on the following: 87 percent knew how to use a "card" catalog: 70 percent knew how to use reference books; and 71 percent knew how to use the Dewey Decimal Classification System. Less than 25 percent of the tutees had had formal instruction in using an on-line catalog, how to use the Library of Congress Classification System, or how to search the Web.

Tutees' Evaluations of Library Instruction Tutors

To obtain information on the Library Instruction Tutoring pilot project the LI Tutors were evaluated by the tutees. During the semester long pilot project, LI Tutors were evaluated by the tutees twice during the semester. Each formal evaluation procedure lasted one week during which the LI Tutors actively sought the tutees' opinions by giving tutees an evaluation form to fill out and drop into a confidential box. Tutees may evaluate a tutor at any time but this evaluation is required by CAPS for two separate weeks during each semester.

Twenty evaluations were received during the pilot project. (See Appendix B for Evaluation Form.) All four LI Tutors were rated in all categories by tutees in the "Agree" or "Strongly Agree" areas. For example, categories included the assessment of tutor friendliness and eagerness to help, tutor preparedness, tutor knowledge of material, tutor listening skills, and the quality of questions asked by tutors. Representational written comments from tutees included the following:

> "The tutor is very helpful and has a lot of patience."

> "She allowed me to ask questions, and let me do my own work."

> "An outstanding tutor. I will recommend him to anyone that needs help."

> "She was a good tutor and I learned a lot about the library from her."

> "The tutor is not at all intimidating—which allows for a relaxed learning environment."

Library Instruction Tutors' Evaluation of the Program

Another important group who provided feedback was the LI Tutors who participated in the pilot project. Their comments on the training programs, ideas for improvement, and suggestions for the future were invaluable.

When asked what the rewards were of being an LI Tutor, they responded with the following statements:

> "It is exciting to help students find that really hard-to-find item."

> "It's my job to search the Internet."

> "I've learned how to do research better by tutoring it to others."

> "Tutees really appreciate us."

> "I like being up-to-date on the latest technologies."

Tutors were also asked about what they have learned about information and libraries. Their comments included:

> "Information and libraries are constantly changing."

> "I learned how computers 'think.' "

"I learned how to do research efficiently and effectively."

"I learned how to manipulate words and vocabulary to find information."

The tutors were also queried regarding the program's strengths and weaknesses. It was unanimous that the greatest strength was the training programs. The LI Tutors appreciated the fact that the training programs provided them with the necessary skills to be successful in their jobs. Suggestions for improving the program included better communication between the LI Tutors and Reference personnel. They also suggested more publicity and advertising of the program to students.

Future Plans for the Library Instruction Tutoring Program

For the pilot project, the one-on-one tutoring appointments were beneficial because they allowed the LI Tutors to work with tutees on an individual basis. The LI Tutors had the opportunity to learn tutoring strategies and also learn, more in-depth, the library content area.

To address the LI Tutors concern about having better communication between Reference personnel and the LI Tutors, several program changes were made. The LI Tutors became involved in assisting with formal Library Instruction workshops and some of their hours were changed to a "drop-in-lab" format.

During the second year of the LITP, tutor duties included serving as assistants during course-related and non-course-related classes taught in the Library. The LI Tutors would be signed out for the workshop as if they had a one-on-one appointment. In the course-related and non-course-related library classes the LI Tutors assisted students while a lecture was being given on research resources by a librarian. LI Tutors assisted students during the session who needed help following along with the lecture. They roamed the class and observed the computer screens during the hands-on sections. This allowed the librarian to continue lecturing without interrupting the whole class to assist one student. The LI Tutors presence also made it more comfortable for the students to make follow-up appointments.

Reference personnel and CAPS also negotiated specific times for LI Tutors to be available in the Reference area for a drop-in-lab situation. The concept of a drop-in lab located in the Reference area helped both parties. The tutors had assigned lab hours and Reference personnel worked closely with the LI Tutors and referred students to the lab. Reference personnel also became more involved with the training program of the LI Tutors.

The LITP is now in its fourth year of operation at the University of New Mexico General Library. The planning process, evaluations, and feedback are fluid and the program is ever changing to meet the needs of the students. This program has assisted hundreds of students over the years and continues to meet UNM students' library research needs using the peer tutoring model.

Chapter 8

Library Instruction Tutoring in K–12 Settings

Teaching library strategies is applicable to settings other than post-secondary institutions. In the secondary environment, the concepts of peer tutoring used at the post-secondary level can easily be applied. At the elementary level, cross-age tutoring is more appropriate. At the middle school level, peer and cross-age tutoring can be practiced. School librarians can take the lead in developing peer or cross-age tutoring programs through collaboration with classroom teachers. Librarians can determine the library literacy skills needed at each grade level or for each curriculum. Information search skills may also be incorporated into computer training. Students can gain computer skills as they research topics using electronic resources and can gain research skills as they learn to use computers. Librarians and teachers have many opportunities to integrate information literacy skills into the curriculum of the school.

In many schools, students serve as library aides, often receiving class credit at the middle and secondary school levels for such work. These students could be trained to serve as tutors, working with other students, both in the library and the classroom. LI Tutors could assist when students work in the library on specific class assignments, either individually or as part of a group project. They could also work in computer labs and in the classroom when information strategies are incorporated into classroom activities. Peer and cross-age tutoring programs exist for a variety of subjects including reading, mathematics, science, and writing, and for competency areas such as computer skills. The effectiveness of these programs is well-documented, and what has been learned from the development of these successful, established programs can be applied to library instruction tutoring programs.

TUTORING IN MIDDLE AND
SECONDARY SCHOOL SETTINGS

Peer tutoring can occur at the secondary level in much the same form as in the post-secondary environment. The pool of potential LI Tutors includes students who work as library aides, assistants in computer classrooms, or members of school clubs and honor societies. CRLA criteria have been applied to secondary tutoring programs. Students who have successfully completed a related course with grades of A or B, and who pass an interview process, are eligible for tutor training and employment. A formal training program, which includes a skills assessment, could be substituted for a related course (see Chapter 3 and Appendix A).

Services provided by LI Tutors at the middle or secondary level could include an overview of the library facility, locations, and collection; introductions to library tools such as the card catalog, print and electronic reference sources, and indexes; and use of the Internet. Tutors could help students locate appropriate sources for specific class assignments such as book reviews, career exploration papers, and research papers in a variety of subject areas. Peer influence may be greatest at the secondary level; the social process of peer interaction supports a program of students teaching other students how to use the library. An informal library-based tutoring program, a general learning tutoring program, and a course-integrated program provide ideas for developing LITPs.

Buboltz and Ling-Louie (1991) reported that installing computers in a junior high school library resulted in the opportunity to observe how students use and experience computer-based technology. Students already interested in technology were the first to use the computers in the library. Without forethought, many of these students became peer tutors, naturally assisting others who were new to computer use and/or experiencing problems with computer use. Buboltz and Ling-Louie also found that students prefer experiences using computer-based technology in small groups rather than in separate areas, such as library carrels. Peer tutors could assist small groups of students in addition to helping individuals. The students who became peer tutors, unfortunately, did not benefit from a training program. The peer tutoring evolved simply from their presence. There was, though, an element of self- or peer-selection concerning the tutors. Some of the technologically advanced students did not become tutors; rather, they became computer hardware and software experts and kept the computers running and loaded with needed software.

Offering course credit for a peer tutoring class is one approach to integrating peer tutoring into the secondary setting. Martino (1993, 1994) described a high school credit course for any students not achieving their potential in the classroom. Tutors and tutees receive credit for enrollment in the course. Tutors are primarily honor students, gifted students, and/or students who have demonstrated effective study strategies in courses for which tutees seek assistance. Tutors are trained to use effective interpersonal skills and communication skills specific to tutoring. Teachers, counselors, and parents refer tutors and tutees. Students can also self-select for participation in the program. During the first year of the program, "The students being tutored showed an average increase gain of 0.67 in their grade-point average; this year [second year] I expect the gains to be even greater" (Martino 1993, 32). The program was so effective, it was expanded to the middle school.

> We targeted [the] peer tutoring class to strive for these goals: improved grades, heightened positive attitude for school, increased sense of achievement, boosted self-confidence, envisioned sense of direction and structure in life and internalized responsibility. To challenge our adolescents to develop the thinking skills necessary for success in other classes, we addressed the following specific academic skills: study techniques and strategies, organizational methods, goal-setting methods, computer-assisted instruction, cooperative learning styles, listening skills, note-taking procedures, speed reading, and word processing (Martino 1994, 56).

Jacobson and Ignacio (1997) experimented with course-integrated instruction in an introductory computer science class taught by a team of teachers and librarians for seventh-, eighth-, and ninth-grade students as well as a few upperclassmen. Information skills were defined, in general, as the gathering and sharing of information. Assignments in the computer science course were designed to support assignments in other courses; for example, most assignments for the seventh and eighth graders were related to research for a science class project. Creating an environment in which students would help other students was one objective of the course design; peer assistance was designed into the program through structured group activities. The authors found that students were not skilled in the role of collaboration, especially in terms of providing feedback to other students.

> Many students simply forgot about sending feedback and, when they were reminded, could not complete it because they had deleted the original messages from their peers. . . . This experience also reminded Jacobson that students were not accustomed to collaborating, especially through e-mail. However, she learned that e-mail use and collaborating with peers were different activities that need to be explicitly taught and scaffolded into the students' culture as well (778).

Potential tutors are abundant in secondary-school settings. Honors programs and honor societies are natural sources of high-achieving students. Also, the sequence of courses offered in middle and high schools allows students to demonstrate proficiency in specific courses taught by specific teachers. For example, students who were successful in Teacher A's seventh-grade English class could be recommended by Teacher A as potential tutors for students currently enrolled in the course.

Students in middle and secondary schools are also potential tutors for elementary school students. At the higher grades, students can demonstrate mastery of elementary school curriculum objectives. During training sessions, these upper-level students would require review, but not new learning, of tutoring program content. Training in tutoring strategies and interpersonal skills would easily complement a review of content.

TUTORING IN ELEMENTARY SCHOOL SETTINGS

In elementary school settings, cross-age tutoring is more prevalent than peer tutoring. In cross-age tutoring relationships, the tutor is usually markedly older than the tutee. For example, fourth- or fifth-grade students would work with first graders, or seventh-grade students would work with third graders. In some cases, high school students work with elementary school students. The nature of the roles played in a tutoring relationship dictate certain levels of maturity and personal development in the tutors so that they can understand and consistently demonstrate specific helping behaviors. For example, it is too great an expectation for six year olds to meet the challenges of tutoring other six year olds. Also, there is a natural interaction among younger students in the elementary classroom, especially in lower grades. Many activities incorporate this natural socialization process; small groups, dyads, reading circles, learning "buddies," and other cooperative learning relationships are used in primary grades. Some element of peer assistance occurs naturally. Reading and writing literacy, as well as computer literacy experiences, are examined to determine the appropriateness of cross-age tutoring in library strategies acquisition. However, cross-age tutoring has been reported as being effective in a variety of disciplines and is not limited to use in reading and computer literacy curriculum.

Reading and Writing Literacy

Cross-age tutoring is commonly used in teaching literacy, especially in teaching specific reading skills. Rekrut (1994) provided six guidelines for tutoring programs in reading: (1) a variety of reading elements are responsive to tutoring; (2) the tutor or tutee may be of any age; (3) tutors are often high achievers but achievers at any level may be well-suited to tutoring; (4) the gender preference is of same-sex partnerships; (5) tutors should be trained in content as well as interpersonal skills, and (6) affective as well as cognitive objectives can be achieved through tutoring (360–61). Rekrut noted that students other than high achievers are often successful as tutors in cross-age programs. For example, when secondary students tutor elementary school students, a student making average grades in eighth grade could be an effective tutor for a fifth-grade student.

In developing guidelines for cross-age reading tutoring in kindergarten, Henriques (1997) focused on five areas: selecting tutors and tutees; training tutors; planning and formatting individual sessions; frequency and length of sessions; and evaluation of the program (44–45). Henriques applied these principles to a cross-age tutoring program for kindergarten students, some of whom spoke English as a second language and were emergent readers. Henriques accepted as potential tutors fourth, fifth, and sixth graders reading at grade level. Tutors completed a questionnaire that solicited background information as well as tutee gender preference. Training included (1) an orientation to the program, including program purpose and goals; (2) instruction in specific literacy strategies, feedback, and reinforcement statements; and (3) specific literacy skills expected for each tutee. The teacher modeled the use of cues in learning to read, and tutors were given examples of appropriate questions and responses. Tutors role played tutoring and reading techniques. Tutors and tutees met twice a week for approximately 30 minutes for three months. Tutees showed substantial increases in emergent reading, writing, and speaking skills. Teachers noted increased participation in class and greater self-confidence on the part of tutees when competing and working with other students. Tutors also reported the experience as positive and made the following comments on an evaluation survey:

- "I felt good inside when she learned all the color words in English."

- "This experience helped me with my little sister."

- "I can feel for my own teacher now."

- "I'd like to be a teacher someday." (45)

Incorporating cross-age tutoring can enhance specific reading programs. In rural Ohio, high school students tutored students in first through third grades as an enhancement to a classwide peer tutoring system. Tutees were chosen because of difficulties with word recognition. High school students, ranging from freshmen to seniors, were nominated to be tutors by study hall teachers. The potential tutors were perceived to have the academic and personal skills needed to be successful tutors. The tutors were trained in the administrative and pedagogical components of the program; tutors and tutees met four days per week for a period of 30–45 minutes. All tutees acquired and maintained a significant number of new sight words, the program's targeted area, as a result of the tutoring sessions. The tutees' teachers also reported positive changes in social and non-targeted academic areas, such as frequency of asking questions in class. Tutors rated the experience as very positive when completing an evaluation survey (Barbetta et al. 1991).

At an elementary school in Texas, fourth-grade students tutored first-grade students in a cross-age literacy program that included not only the traditional tutoring relationship, but also included tutors and tutees working together to acquire information from library sources, reading activities, and book-writing skills. The traditional tutoring activities focused on spelling skills. The tutor and tutee became partners by practicing the first grader's spelling skills and by having the fourth grader assess the first grader's progress. Fourth graders helped teachers find information concerning topics covered in the first-grade class by accessing library books and encyclopedias. The tutors compiled and/or created poems, books, riddles, and word games concerning the topic. These materials became part of the first-grade library during a particular unit of study. Tutors selected appropriate library books and prepared to read the books aloud to a tutee. As readers, the tutors asked and answered questions about the material. The reading was recorded, and the recordings were kept in the first-grade classroom listening center for regular use. The fourth-grade tutors also collaborated with the first-grade students to coauthor books. First graders drew pictures and then dictated sentences to the fourth graders relating to the pictures. The fourth graders compiled all the pictures and sentences into a class book. Fourth graders also wrote their auto-biographies and interviewed a first grader for a biography. These books were illustrated and presented to the first graders. Teachers reported that the tutors and tutees improved their skills in a variety of areas. Tutors become more proficient in oral reading, expressive reading, and writing. Tutees gained skills in spelling, reading, writing, and cooperative social skills. Teachers and parents observed increased self-esteem in tutors and tutees as all students took pride in the creative accomplishments of the program. "Children are great motivators for other children and a cross-age literacy program makes becoming literate a friendly, natural process as children work together. Reading and writing should not be solitary acts of copying or sounding out, but rather should be fun, group activities" (DeRita and Weaver 1991, 248).

Topping (1998) suggested a developmental hierarchy for tutoring reading at the kindergarten through third-grade levels. Topping addressed the issue of volunteer tutors, including but not limited to student-to-student tutoring. The hierarchy, however, is a framework that can be appropriately used as a foundation for cross-age, student-based reading programs. The hierarchy from lowest to highest levels is "listen, talk with, help choose books, book skills, read to, help make books, read with, repeated readings, help read independently, discuss reading" (48).

Computer Literacy

With the introduction of computers into schools during the past two decades, teaching computer literacy has become an integral component of elementary school curriculum. M. Ellen Jay (1998) proposed computer literacy skills for kindergarten through fifth-grade students and urged collaboration among library media specialists, classroom teachers, and computer lab coordinators to create opportunities for skill development. Cross-age tutoring programs have been successful in helping students acquire computer literacy.

In a small Midwestern elementary school, fourth graders helped second graders acquire computer skills. The tutors were fourth-grade students who demonstrated a mastery of all the objectives of the second-grade computer literacy curriculum. Tutees were second-grade students who did not demonstrate a mastery of the second-grade computer literacy curriculum. The tutees demonstrated some computer game-playing skills, but none of the tutees demonstrated keyboarding or word processing skills. Tutors participated in training sessions covering keyboarding, problem-solving, and word processing competence as well as interpersonal tutoring strategies. Follow-up support sessions were scheduled; however, tutors did not sign up for the sessions, an indicator, as perceived by teachers, of their comfort in the tutoring role. After ten 30-minute tutoring sessions, all tutees were able to effectively use the keyboard and the problem-solving and word processing programs presented and practiced during the sessions. Tutees were also able to identify parts of the computer, use appropriate terms when talking about computers, and demonstrate appropriate care and use of computers. Benefits to tutors were not assessed (Newell 1996).

Students in a high school English and computer applications course and students in a second-/third-grade classroom in a suburban Seattle school district successfully collaborated in a writing and computer cross-age tutoring program. The elementary students created original stories that the high school tutors entered into the computer. The tutors interviewed the elementary students for a biographical addition to the story. When composing the biographical statement, the tutors demonstrated writing skills with an emphasis on grammar, punctuation, and spelling. The tutors and tutees also researched potential summer activities by researching a favorite place within the greater Seattle geographical area. The information was entered into a database and a guide was produced (Orwig 1995).

INFORMATION LITERACY
SKILLS FOR K–12

When creating a library instruction tutoring program for elementary, middle, and secondary school students, the library skills content must be determined. Arany (1992) noted that "a new theory of library instruction seems to be evolving. This theory broadens the scope of library skills and clearly emphasizes the application of the higher level thinking skills to the utilization of information" (19). Arany outlined information skills needed for grades three through six using five skill sets as the structure for developing the curriculum: locational skills, reference and research skills, interpretation and communication skills, audiovisual skills, and computer skills. Students progress through each of the five skill sets developmentally from grades three through five. At grade six, research and reference skills are emphasized; the assumption is that students have achieved expected competence in the other five categories at the end of the fifth grade.

McGuire (1998) proposed grade-level Library Media Center skills for kindergarten through fifth grade. Some skills are expected at all grade levels including locating the library, asking for assistance, replacing books, selecting appropriate books, and returning books. Other skills are developmental: at grade five, for example, students are taught to locate books according to decimal systems, to re-shelve books, and to operate selected audiovisual equipment. At grade four, students "assist younger readers with basic research" (23). This element of cross-age tutoring appears in McGuire's guidelines without the establishment of a formal cross-age tutoring program. McGuire also provided library media instruction in terms of reading level. Browsing and finding checklists skills were developed for emergent, early, early-intermediate, intermediate, experienced, and proficient readers.

Eisenberg and Berkowitz (1988) proposed the "Big Six Skills" as a model for school library instruction. The six skills are Task Definition, Information-Seeking Strategies, Location and Access, Use of Information, Synthesis, and Evaluation. When taught in the context of classroom assignments, the six skills provide the basis for information-literate students. In 1997, Eisenberg and Berkowitz integrated technology skills into the Big Six Skills model and continued to advance the collaboration between school librarian and classroom teacher.

> When we reflect on integrating technology skills into teaching and learning, we realize that it is not necessary to change the fundamentals of quality instruction or the information problem-solving perspective that is at the heart of the Big Six Skills approach. The implementation of the Big Six approach develops students' problem-solving, complex thinking and information management abilities. It also enables students to become comfortable with technology and understand that technology is simply a tool to help them perform their work (22).

Craver (1997) identified universal electronic literacy concepts that students must master to be information literate in an electronic environment. "Students need a basic understanding of the structure of electronic information, computer indexes, keyword and subject searching, and the use of thesauri to enable them to use a variety of electronic resources successfully" (1). With the advent of the electronic information environment, it is no longer sufficient to know how to use particular information and search tools. Students must understand the organization of the information and the rationale for various search strategies before they can make meaningful and productive research decisions. Using an active learning approach, Craver provided sample lessons and suggested assignments for each of 11 electronic literacy concepts. The assignments can be integrated into course content or used as library-centered experiences.

By 1994, 27 states had adopted information literacy skills for public school students. Although specific skills and emphasis on those skills may vary from state to state, establishing guidelines is at least a first step in establishing standards that will create information literate students as part of the educational process ("If we had information standards," 1994).

In 1998, the American Library Association published *Information Power: Building Partnerships for Learning*, a joint work of the Association of School Librarians and the Association for Educational Communications and Technology. Included in the publication are nine information literacy standards for student learning. The standards are organized into the three areas of information literacy, independent learning, and social responsibility. Each standard includes levels of proficiency, associated grade-level activities, and examples of content area standards.

PROPOSED MODELS OF LIBRARY INSTRUCTION TUTORING PROGRAMS

Documentation on cross-age tutoring's success at the elementary and middle school levels and peer and/or cross-age tutoring's success at the middle and secondary school levels provides an important element for the establishment of formal LITPs. Tutors and tutees benefit academically and personally from the tutoring relationship (Gartner and Riessman 1994). Tutoring provides structure and flexibility in meeting the individual needs of the learner. In addition, preliminary research to identify effective teaching methods in the digital library environment indicates that a variety of methods are needed and should be used to individualize instruction. Jacobson and Ignacio (1997) found that no one theoretical model was sufficient for teaching all students.

> Strategies also need to be differentiated and tailored to each student's particular needs. The students in this situation learned how to search and evaluate information in a classroom setting. Yet the help they received was also personalized through feedback on assignments, in-class coaching, and out-of-class conferencing. User-friendly digital library interfaces are not enough; skilled mediation and intervention will always be necessary (793).

Formal library instruction tutoring programs provide the opportunity to apply an effective instructional strategy in an environment that requires personalization.

Curriculum/Course-Integrated Tutoring Model

Research skills are merged with subject area content to create a meaningful learning experience for students when information literacy and library use skills are integrated into the school's curriculum. Integrated approaches keep information literacy and library use skills from being viewed as skills detached from content and application. Integrated approaches to the teaching and learning of research strategies provide opportunities for collaboration between school librarians and teachers and opportunities for student-to-student tutoring.

Pawlowski and Troutman (1991) described a curriculum-integrated approach to teaching high school sophomores the mechanics of searching electronic and print sources. Instruction begins in English classes and continues with an assignment in biology classes related to science fair projects. The classroom teacher and library media specialists work together to develop a search strategy that the students will use. Students use that strategy, with reinforcement, in the classroom and the library over five class periods to conduct a preliminary search on their science fair topic. Returning to the library weekly for several months, students continue to gather data for their projects. This year-long sophomore approach to searching information sources concludes with the students completing a research paper in their English classes on a current topic of interest. Instruction in the use of audiovisual production techniques is included in this final project. "The classroom teacher and library staff continue to function as an instruction team, helping students document their resources and making adjustments for different levels of student ability" (15). The use of peer tutors would enhance this instruction model. Junior and senior students who had successfully completed the science fair projects and research papers could become part of the instructional team assisting sophomores with current-year assignments. More students would receive individual attention, and sophomore students would have peers as models in addition to learning from teachers and media specialists.

In *Information Power*, tutoring is a presented as a program for fostering community and school collaboration. Individuals in the community could volunteer as tutors; students could also be encouraged to participate in community projects. Although this link between the school and the community in terms of community projects is very valuable for connecting students with real-life experiences, it ignores the peer-helping component of learning. Library media specialists are called on to create learning communities within and beyond the school. The learning community within the school includes students, teachers, and administrators. Collaborative efforts should include peer or cross-age tutoring as a component of an effective learning community.

Potential tutors are those students who either have successfully completed the course(s) targeted for integrated research instruction or who have demonstrated effective research skills in another academic setting—school or community projects or honor society activities, for example.

Teacher and librarian collaboration in the selection of tutors would further enhance the environment of partnership essential to course-integrated curricula. The criteria for selecting tutors could include demonstration of the specific skills included in course objectives, as well as recommendations and pre-hire interviews. Before tutoring begins, training would include a review of the course structure, objectives, and assignments, as well as the interpersonal and communications skills necessary for establishing effective tutoring relationships. During the instruction and tutoring period, training would focus on research and content skills with the opportunity to resolve any relationship problems. A tutor coordinator is needed for the project for program oversight, problem-solving, and evaluation. The coordinator could be a member of the instruction team or another professional with the appropriate background, such as a counselor. In a school with established tutoring programs, program organization might be facilitated through a school-based tutoring coordinator. Other tutoring programs could also be the source of experienced tutors.

Library-Centered Tutoring Model

Even though the course-integrated approach to instruction is the preferred model for providing meaningful context for acquiring research strategies, its application is not practical in all schools or, when applied, does not include all students. An alternative or additional approach is training library student aides as library tutors. As previously reported, Buboltz and Ling-Louie (1991) found that some peer assistance occurred naturally when computers were installed in a junior high school library. Students interested in computers were drawn to the library and became tutors to less-experienced computer users.

School libraries that have library aides could add the interpersonal and communications skills needed for effective tutoring relationships to the training program of those students. The training for library aides should already incorporate search strategies, use of library tools, and print and non-print sources. Tutors could assist students when classes come to the library for specific projects and when students work independently on those projects. In school library settings that include computer labs, library aides might also serve as computer literacy tutors, helping students with computer-assisted instruction programs and/or software packages for word processing, for example. If classrooms include computer access, these library tutors could be assigned to classes when computer and/or research skills are practiced. Working with individuals or small groups, working in the library or classroom, library-based tutors could enhance the teaching and learning environment for students, teachers, and librarians.

GENERAL PROGRAM
DEVELOPMENT GUIDELINES

General program guidelines provide a useful framework for creating a K–12 library instruction tutoring program. Miller et al. (1993) proposed four components for effective peer tutoring programs: planning, training, monitoring and evaluation, and problem-solving. Planning involves identifying skills supported by tutoring, selecting materials used by tutors and tutees, selecting a programmatic tutoring schedule, and structuring the tutor–tutee interaction to enhance effectiveness. Training provides an introduction to the tutoring process with a rationale for each step, modeling of the process, and opportunities to practice tutoring in a coaching environment. Miller et al. advocated a very structured training model and noted that, although training takes time,

> the benefits of conducting these step-by-step procedures in a planned way are significant. Most important, instruction is occurring at a rapid pace and in a format that students enjoy. Feedback is also occurring more frequently than the teacher is typically able to provide, suggesting that students will spend more time practicing correct answers. In summary, structured training can have payoffs well worth the time and energy expended to learn the procedures (16–17).

Monitoring and evaluation, as described by Miller et al., included monitoring tutor–tutee interactions at the beginning and the end of tutoring sessions. The beginning and ending of sessions provide organization to the tutoring process. Monitoring tutor–tutee interactions provides opportunities for the teacher to give feedback as the tutoring is taking place. In less than a minute, tutors and tutees can be praised for good work and can be corrected when problems in the process occur; for example, when the tutor does not wait long enough for a response from the tutee. Evaluation is the assessment of the outcomes of tutoring. Are tutees learning the material? Are they able to perform operations on their own? Evaluation tools include formal and informal quizzes and tests, direct observations, worksheets, and any other suitable measure for understanding and applying the content of tutoring sessions. Monitoring and evaluation lead into the fourth component of a tutoring program—problem-solving. At this stage, discrepancies between planning and application are noted. Changes to the program plan, training program, and/or assessment devices are made. These changes can include changes in the tutor selection and/or assignment process, changes in content supported by tutoring, development of additional tutoring materials, additions or deletions to training modules, and development of assessment tools.

Tansy et al. (1996) included several other areas of importance in establishing peer and cross-age tutoring programs. They were interested in giving school counselors important roles in developing tutoring programs, including serving as program coordinators. Included in program development activities are cost effectiveness (administrative support), and school readiness (attitudes, resources, and training), as well as preparation for students (tutor selection and training), teachers (content selection and training), and parents (understanding and consent). As the program is implemented, the selection of tutors is important in providing opportunities for program success.

> Each type of tutor offers a degree of assurance that the program will be accepted. The academically accomplished tutor will bring mastery of the subject matter to the tutoring session, the influential peer will popularize the program with the peer culture, and the "at risk" tutor will provide evidence that the program is of benefit to those who tutor (20).

Tansy et al. also discussed the need to give students incentives to participate in the program, as either tutors or tutees. This is particularly important in cross-age tutoring programs in which tutors and tutees will have little or no personal connection before the tutoring begins. In addition to incentives, such as notices of achievement and elective course credit for middle school and high school tutors, they suggested that opportunities for "personal reflection and discussion of students' experiences in the program are especially useful" (26). In general, the principles outlined in Tansy et al. for counselor-coordinated programs are similar to those suggested by Miller et al. for teacher-coordinated programs.

CONSIDERATIONS FOR ESTABLISHING A PROGRAM

Library instruction tutoring programs are appropriate for K–12 settings. Tutoring programs for reading, writing, and computer literacy have been successful; these content areas are directly related to information literacy. Students benefit from being tutored and from being tutors. Peer and cross-age tutoring can be implemented, with cross-age tutoring more prevalent in the lower grades and peer tutoring more easily implemented in the higher grades. Information literacy standards are available for students at each grade level and can be taught as stand-alone skills or as part of a school's curriculum.

Planning

When establishing a library instruction peer or cross-age tutoring program, the school learning environment and general principles of program development will dictate program direction. Perhaps the most important planning factor is identifying course-related tutoring opportunities. If course-related library instruction is the model used at the school, library instruction tutoring can become an element of the already established interaction between the school librarian and students in the classroom. For example, if the librarian introduces second-grade students to specific elements of research, tutors (perhaps fourth or fifth graders) can be trained to provide individual assistance to those students as they practice and gain research skills.

If no opportunities for course-related library instruction can be identified, a library-centered approach can be implemented. Students who work as library aides are trained to provide library information strategies tutoring when students come to the library to learn how to access and use resources. Students may come to the library individually, as part of a class, or as part of a study group. If the library is used as a study hall, the presence of library instruction tutors enhances the learning environment.

Course-integrated or library-centered approaches should involve the school librarian and teachers. A program created only by the school librarian, without collaborating with teachers, may result in an isolated program, limited to the few students who work in the library and/or those who express an independent interest in library information use. An isolated program may also mean competition rather than collaboration for use of limited resources.

Another factor to consider is whether the school has an established tutoring program for related skills such as reading, writing, and/or computer literacy. We suggest that if a successful program exists, efforts should be made to integrate library information strategies into the established program. Existing tutoring programs for reading, writing, and/or computer literacy also provide a pool of potential tutors.

The location of computers in the school will also influence the structure of the library instruction tutoring program. Schools with up-to-date computer resources in the library will benefit from a library-based tutoring model, even if tutoring is also tied to course objectives. However, in schools with small computer pods in each classroom or with computer labs separate from the library and classrooms, collaborative programs are essential for success.

Training

Training for tutors is the key component for any program. Training must include content and elements of the tutoring relationship and should be organized into initial training and on-going training modules. Initially, seeing appropriate behaviors modeled and having opportunities to practice those behaviors with constructive feedback are powerful training strategies. Guidelines, scheduling, supervision, paperwork, and other organizational matters should also be included in the initial training. On-going training includes opportunities for discussion and feedback for improving tutoring skills and for problem-solving while the tutoring program is operational.

Training for tutees and parents may be included in some training programs. In programs that assign a student to a tutor for a specific period of time, the student may need to learn the expectations of the tutee role as well as how progress will be assessed. Parents need to be involved, at the very least, when students have tutoring-related homework. In general, parents need to understand the purposes of tutoring, their child's role in the process, and any instructional support they need to provide with training for that support.

Evaluation

Evaluation occurs at several levels. First, the process should be monitored. Whether tutors serve as assistants to teachers and/or librarians in the classroom, provide individual instruction in the library, or are assigned to a particular student for a pre-determined time period, the content and structure of tutoring interactions should be monitored. The primary focus of this monitoring is whether or not tutors are implementing the tutoring model practiced during training. Feedback can be provided as part of the on-going training program. Tutors also play an active role in monitoring, with a focus on whether they encountered situations not covered by training or whether some training components should be reviewed.

Second, an assessment of tutoring outcomes must be made. Are students learning the content of tutoring? Are they better library information users? What is the quality of materials found during a search process? Are tutees more independent in their use of library resources? The goals and objectives of the tutoring program are established during the planning phase. Evaluation determines whether those goals and objectives are met.

Third, the information gathered during monitoring and assessment activities should be incorporated into the planning and training elements of the program. Successes should be replicated and weaknesses strengthened.

Checklist for Establishing a
Library Instruction Tutoring Program

Assess possibilities for program structure. Are there opportunities for course-related instruction? Which teachers incorporate some level of library use into class assignments? Which teachers are open to collaboration and team teaching? Do goals and objectives dictate the need for cross-age tutoring or for peer tutoring? Will tutoring take place within the classroom—tutors providing support as students practice information literacy skills? Or will tutoring take place outside the classroom, either through open practice sessions or assigned tutor–tutee relationships? If the program is library-centered, when will students access tutoring services? Will tutors provide support as students practice using resources?

Determine sources of cross-age or peer tutors. Are there existing tutoring programs that might provide a pool of potential tutors? When taking a course-related approach, are there easily identifiable students who succeeded in the course the previous year(s)? Are there library aides who can be trained as tutors to support either course-related or library-centered tutoring programs?

Create training modules for initial and on-going training. What information is needed for tutors as they begin tutoring—in areas such as logistics, content, and communications skills? How will improvement be made during the implementation of the program? Do tutees and parents need to participate?

Develop monitoring strategies. How, when, and by whom will monitoring take place? How will information be incorporated into on-going training? How will adjustments be made if needed?

Assess tutoring outcomes. Have program goals and objectives been met? If not, how can goals and objectives be modified? If goals and objectives were met, should they be expanded or enhanced? How will assessment information be incorporated into planning and training? Were assessment activities appropriate or are changes needed?

REFERENCES

Arany, Ruth Ann. 1992. Creating reasonably independent lifelong library and information users. *Indiana Media Journal* 14: 19–24.

Association of School Librarians and Association for Educational Communications and Technology. 1998. *Information power: Building partnerships for learning.* Chicago: American Library Association.

Barbetta, Patricia M., April D. Miller, Mary T. Peters, Timothy E. Heron, and Lessie L. Cochran. 1991. Tugmate: A cross-age tutoring program to teach sight vocabulary. *Education and Treatment of Children* 14 (1): 19–37.

Buboltz, Dale, and Ruby Ling-Louie. 1991. On the trail of technology. *The Book Report* 10 (3): 13.

Craver, Kathleen. 1997. *Teaching electronic literacy.* Westport, Conn.: Greenwood Press.

DeRita, Carol, and Susan Weaver. 1991. Cross-age literacy program. *Reading Improvement* 28 (4): 244–248.

Eisenberg, Michael, and Robert E. Berkowitz. 1988. Curriculum initiative: An agenda and strategy for library media programs. Norwood, N.J.: Ablex.

———. 1997. Teaching research skills electronically. *Book Report* 16 (2): 15–22.

Gartner, Audrey J., and Frank Riessman. 1994. Tutoring helps those who give, those who receive. *Educational Leadership* 52 (3): 58–61.

Henriques, Marlene E. 1997. Increasing literacy among kindergartners though cross-age training. *Young Children* 52 (4): 42–47.

If we had information standards, what would they be? 1994. *School Library Media Activities Monthly* 10 (5): 49–50.

Jacobson, Frances F., and Emily N. Ignacio. 1997. Teaching reflection: Information seeking and evaluation in a digital library environment. *Library Trends* 45 (4): 771–802.

Jay, M. Ellen. 1998. Developing computer literacy skills in schools with library media centers, classroom and lab access. *School Library Media Activities Monthly* 14 (10): 27–30.

Martino, Louis R. 1993. When students help students. *The Executive Educator* 15 (1): 31–32.

———. 1994. Peer tutoring Classes for Young Adolescents: A cost-effective strategy. *Middle School Journal* 25 (4): 55–58.

McGuire, Patience Lea. 1998. Developmentally appropriate library media skills instruction. *School Library Media Activities Monthly* 14 (6): 22–28.

Miller, Linda J., Frank W. Kohler, Helen Ezell, Kathryn Hoel Ezell, and Phillip S. Strain. 1993. Winning with peer tutoring. *Preventing School Failure* 37 (3): 14–18.

Newell, Florence M. 1996. Effects of a cross-age tutoring program on computer literacy learning of second-grade students. *Journal of Research on Computing in Education* 28 (3): 346–358.

Orwig, Ann H. 1995. Bridging the ages with help from technology. *Technology and Learning* 16 (1): 26–33.

Pawlowski, Connie, and Patsy Troutman. 1991. Blending print & electronic sources. *The Book Report* 10 (3): 14–17.

Rekrut, Martha D. 1994. Peer and cross-age tutoring: The lessons of research. *Journal of Reading* 37 (5): 356–362.

Tansy, Michael, Maryann Santos de Barona, Jeffries McWhirter, and D. Scott Herrmann. 1996. Peer and cross-age tutoring programs. *Guidance and Counselling* [On-line], 12 (1): 21–24. Available: ESBCOhost/Academic Search FullTEXT Elite/Accession #9707080871 [1998, December 30].

Topping, Keith. 1998. Effective tutoring in America Reads: A reply to Wasik. *The Reading Teacher* 52 (1): 42–50.

ADDITIONAL READINGS

Allen, Vernon, ed. 1976. *Children as teachers: Theory and research on tutoring.* New York: Academic Press.

Berliner, David, and Ursula Casanova. 1986. How to make cross-age tutoring work. *Instructor* 95 (9): 14–15.

Bohning. Gerry. 1982. A resource guide for planning, implementing and evaluating peer and cross-age tutoring. *Reading Improvement* 19 (4): 274–278.

Boloz, Sigmund A., and Donna H. Muri. 1994. Supporting emergent literacy is everyone's responsibility. *The Reading Teacher* 47 (5): 388–399.

Cohen, P., J. Kulik, and C. Kulik. 1982. Educational outcomes of tutoring: A meta-analysis of findings. *American Educational Research Journal* 19 (2): 237–248.

Goodlad, Sinclair, ed. 1998. *Mentoring and tutoring by students.* London: Kogan Page.

Kuhlthau, C. C. 1988. Developing a model of the library search process: Cognitive and affective aspects. *RQ* 28 (2): 232–242.

Levin, Henry M., G. V. Glass, and G. R. Meister. 1984. Cost-effectiveness of four educational interventions. Stanford: Stanford University, Institute for Research on Educational Finance and Governance. ERIC Document 246 533.

Mavrogenes, Nancy A. and Nancy D. Galen. 1979. Cross-age tutoring: Why and how. *Journal of Reading* 22 (4): 345–353.

Norris, Cathleen A. 1994. Computing and the classroom: Teaching the at-risk student. *The Computing Teacher*, 2: 12–14.

Wasik, Barbara A., and Robert E. Slavin. 1993. Preventing early reading failure with one-to-one tutoring: A review of five programs. *Reading Research Quarterly* 28 (2): 178–200.

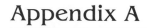

The College Reading and Learning Association International Tutor Training Certification Program

FACT SHEET

The International Tutor Training Certification Program

- Is sponsored by the College Reading and Learning Association

- Began in 1989

- Certifies programs at three levels

- Requires 10 hours of training and 25 hours of tutoring experience for each certification level

- Costs $50 for the initial one-year certification at one, two, or all levels

- Costs $25 for recertification for three years and $50 for five years

- Provides professional standards for tutor training

- Rewards tutors

- Establishes credibility for tutoring programs

- Is endorsed by the National Association for Developmental Education and Commission XVI, Academic Support in Higher Education, of the American College Personnel Association

- Has filled over 940 requests for information and application packets This number changes daily

- More than 400 programs had been certified as of June 2000; 36 had been de-certified; 12 were pending certification

- Produced a handbook in 1995 entitled *The College Reading and Learning Association's Tutor Training Handbook* that is available for $20 or on-line at www.crla.net

- Is coordinated by Gladys R. Shaw, U.T. El Paso, Tutoring and Learning Ctr., 300 Library, El Paso, TX 79968, (915) 747-5366, (fax) (915) 747-5486, e-mail gshaw@utep.edu and Robin Melton, U.T. Arlington, Box 19509, Arlington, TX 76019, (817) 273-2617, (fax) (817) 272-3370

CRLA TUTOR CERTIFICATION . . . Consider the POSSIBILITIES!

CRLA Tutor Certification offers numerous benefits for individual tutors, tutorial coordinators, and programs. The following is a *partial* list of the opportunities/benefits that are possible with CRLA Tutor Certification:

1. Develop a super tutoring program from scratch by utilizing certification guidelines, *The CRLA Tutor Training Handbook*, and the experience of other professionals attending CRLA conferences.

2. Utilize allotted time for development of an individual certification plan to carefully rethink your whole existing tutorial program, an opportunity for a fresh perspective.

3. Using CRLA guidelines, organize separate training sessions into a coherent curriculum and possibly a credit course.

4. Create a spirit of teamwork in your department by involving colleagues in tutor training curriculum design, actual tutor training, and tutor evaluation.

5. Generate interest in the community about your program by giving a press release to local and campus newspapers about your CRLA Certified Program. Include CRLA CERTIFIED TUTORS on all of your program advertisements.

6. Secure greater student and faculty confidence and respect for your tutorial staff and program.

7. Attract attention and interest among other tutorial services on campus. May stimulate interaction for the betterment of both programs such as working together on training.

8. Attract highly motivated tutors with CRLA Certification credentials and extensive training.

9. Tie wage rates to CRLA Certification levels in order to provide incentive for additional training and experience. This also helps with retention of tutors.

10. Involve upper level tutors in developing and/or conducting segments of lower level tutor training. This creates excitement and motivation for ALL tutors and staff.

11. Honor certified tutors by hosting a ceremony/party in their honor. Invite all tutors, selected faculty, and staff.

12. Emphasize the transferability of CRLA Tutor Certification to other certifying colleges and universities. In other words, a Level I Certificate earned at one institution would be recognized at another.

13. Encourage tutors to add CRLA Tutor Certification to their resumes and to talk about their training and experience in job interviews.

14. Add to your own resume with items such as authored certification proposal, developed and conducted tutor training, and maintained certification records.

By Robin Melton
Co-Chair of the ITTCP
12/1/97

COLLEGE READING AND LEARNING ASSOCIATION'S CERTIFICATION OF TUTOR PROGRAMS

PURPOSE, PROCEDURES, & GUIDELINES

1. *PURPOSE*

    The purpose of establishing a series of tutoring certificates is twofold. First, it allows tutors to receive recognition and positive reinforcement for their successful work from an international organization, CRLA. Secondly, the certificates help set up a standard for the minimum skills and training a tutor needs to be successful.

2. *PROCEDURES FOR HAVING A PROGRAM CERTIFIED*

    A. An institution that wishes to have a tutor program or programs certified should designate one individual *per tutor program or group of tutor programs* who will act as liaison between the CRLA International Tutor Certification Committee (ITCP) and that institution's program or programs;

    B. The designated individual should complete and submit three sets of the application packets for **each program to be certified** consisting of 1) CRLA Application for Certification of Tutor Program; 2) the necessary "Verification of Tutor Program" forms; 3) plus the necessary documentation concerning how the institution's tutor program(s) meets the criteria outlined in "CRLA's REQUIREMENTS FOR CERTIFICATION OF TUTOR PROGRAMS" to the CRLA ITCP;

    C. One set of the application packet and documentation will remain on file with the CRLA ITCP Chair.

3. *GENERAL INFORMATION*

    A. Once an institution's tutor program is certified, that **program** will receive a certificate and be authorized to issue individual CRLA tutoring certificates. A master copy of the individual certificate for each certified level will also be included.

    B. There are three levels of individual certification: Regular/Level 1; Advanced/Level 2; and Master/Level 3. Certification can be requested for Level 1 only or for more than one level such as Level 1 and Level 2, or Levels 1, 2, and 3 at the same time for a program if appropriate training is in place.

C. The initial institutional certification will be for a one year period.

D. There will be one renewal certification for three years. **(New levels for the same program and new programs cannot be combined with or included in recertification applications. Only the original program certified for one year will be recertified for three.)** The three-year renewal fee is $25.

E. After the three-year renewal certification there will be recertifications for five years. **(New levels for the same program and new programs cannot be combined with or included in recertification applications. Only the original program certified for one year will be recertified for three, five, etc.)** The five-year renewal fee is $50.

F. During the initial certification period certification of tutors will be retroactive for one year from date of certification.

G. Certification dates are from July 1 through June 30 regardless of when it is granted. Through December the certification date is the prior July 1. After January 1, it is the following July 1.

4. *IMPORTANT NOTES:*

CRLA certifies programs not individual tutors. In other words, CRLA certifies that a particular tutor training program is qualified to issue CRLA certificates to individual tutors at a certain level or levels. The responsibility for tracking an individual tutor's training, tutoring hours, etc. and issuing certificates when a tutor qualifies lies with the tutoring program certified. Each institution must keep a record for each of its certified tutors that is subject to review by CRLA if the need arises.

COLLEGE READING & LEARNING ASSOCIATION'S

REQUIREMENTS FOR
CERTIFICATION OF TUTOR PROGRAMS

I. *REQUIREMENTS FOR REGULAR/LEVEL 1 CERTIFICATION*

A. *AMOUNT/DURATION OF TUTOR TRAINING:*
(one or more of the following).

1. Minimum of 10 hours of tutor training

2. A quarter/semester tutor training course

3. A quarter/semester of tutor training (non-course work)

B. *MODES OF TUTOR TRAINING*

1. Classroom and/or workshop instruction
PLUS two or more of the following

2. Tutor training videotapes

3. Conferences with tutor trainer/supervisor

4. Special tutor projects

5. Other

C. *AREAS/TOPICS TO BE COVERED IN TUTOR TRAINING: A mini-*
mum of eight (8) of the following topics should be covered in Level 1
training. The exact amount of time devoted to each topic may vary.

1. Definition of tutoring and tutor responsibilities

2. Basic tutoring guidelines

3. Techniques for successfully beginning and ending a tutor
session

4. Some basic Tutoring Do's

5. Some basic Tutoring Don'ts

6. Role Modeling

7. Setting Goals/Planning

8. Communication Skills

9. Active listening and paraphrasing

10. Referral Skills

11. Study Skills

12. Critical Thinking Skills

13. Compliance with the Ethics and Philosophy of the Tutor
Program

14. Modeling problem-solving

15. Other (please specify)

D. *REQUIRED TUTORING EXPERIENCE*

25 hours of actual tutoring

E. *TUTOR SELECTION CRITERIA*

1. Interview plus written approval of a content/skill instructor *AND/OR*

2. Interview plus endorsement of tutor trainer/supervisor *PLUS* at least one of the following:

3. Grade of "A" or "B" in subject content being tutored

4. Documented experience equivalent to #3

F. *TUTOR EVALUATION CRITERIA*

1. A formal/informal evaluation process is in place

2. Formal/informal evaluation occurs on a regular basis

3. The results of the evaluation process are made known to the tutors

II. **REQUIREMENTS FOR ADVANCED/LEVEL 2 CERTIFICATION (NOTE: TUTOR MUST HAVE COMPLETED LEVEL 1 CERTIFICATION REQUIREMENTS).**

A. *AMOUNT/DURATION OF TUTOR TRAINING: (one or more of the following).*

1. Minimum of 10 hours of tutor training beyond Level 1 (a minimum of 20 cumulative hours of tutor training)

2. A second quarter/semester tutor training course

3. A second quarter/semester of tutor training (non-course work)

B. *MODES OF TUTOR TRAINING*

1. Classroom and/or workshop instruction *PLUS* two or more of the following

2. Tutor training videotapes

3. Conference with tutor trainer/supervisor

4. Special tutor projects

5. Other

C. *AREAS/TOPICS TO BE COVERED IN TUTOR TRAINING:*
In addition to reviewing the topics covered in Level 1 a minimum of four (4) of the following topics should be covered in Level 2 training. The exact amount of time devoted to each topic may vary.

1. Review of *Level 1* topics

2. Use of probing questions

   3. Characteristics of adult learners/learning styles

   4. Cultural awareness and inter-cultural communications

   5. Identifying and using resources

   6. Tutoring in specific skill/subject areas

   7. Record keeping/documentation

   8. Other (please specify)

D. *REQUIRED TUTORING EXPERIENCE*
    25 additional hours of actual tutoring after completion of all Level 1 requirements (a minimum of 50 cumulative hours of actual tutoring)

E. *TUTOR SELECTION CRITERIA*

   1. Met at Level 1

F. *TUTOR EVALUATION CRITERIA*

   1. Met at Level 1

III. *REQUIREMENTS FOR MASTER/LEVEL 3 CERTIFICATION (NOTE: TUTOR MUST HAVE COMPLETED LEVEL 1 AND 2 CERTIFICATION REQUIREMENTS).*

A. *AMOUNT/DURATION OF TUTOR TRAINING:*
    (one or more of the following).

   1. Minimum of 10 hours of tutor training beyond Level 2 (a minimum of 30 cumulative hours of tutor training)

   2. A third quarter/semester tutor training course

   3. A third quarter/semester of tutor training (non-course work)

B. *MODES OF TUTOR TRAINING*

   1. Classroom and/or workshop instruction
       PLUS two or more of the following

   2. Tutor training videotapes

   3. Conferences with tutor trainer/supervisor

   4. Special tutor projects

   5. Other

C. *AREAS/TOPICS TO BE COVERED IN TUTOR TRAINING:*
    In addition to reviewing the topics covered in Level 1 and 2 a minimum
    of four (4) of the following topics should be covered in Level 3 training.
    The exact amount of time devoted to each topic may vary.

    1. Review of Level 1 and Level 2 topics
    2. Assertiveness training
    3. How to tutor/deal with target populations
    4. How to administer and interpret a learning style inventory
    5. Structuring the learning experience
    6. Training and supervising other tutors (supervisory skills)
    7. Group management skills (group interaction and group dynamics)
    8. Other (please specify)

D. *REQUIRED TUTORING EXPERIENCE*
    25 additional hours of actual tutoring after completion of all Level
    1 and Level 2 requirements (a minimum of 75 cumulative hours of
    actual tutoring)

E. *TUTOR SELECTION CRITERIA*
    1. Met at Level 1

F. *TUTOR EVALUATION CRITERIA*
    1. Met at Level 1

COLLEGE READING AND LEARNING ASSOCIATION

TUTOR TRAINING PROGRAM
CERTIFICATION SELF-ASSESSMENT

(Please complete prior to Application for Certification and use it in conjunction with the document, "Requirements for Certification of Tutor Programs. This assessment will help you determine whether or not your program meets certification requirements before you apply. If applying for more than one level, you will want to complete the assessment for each level for which you are seeking certification).

A. Amount of Training for Level _____
   REQUIRED: 10 HRS.
   We have in place _____ hrs.

   How can we document? (Ex.: Course Syllabus, Training Syllabus):

B. Modes
   REQUIRED: AT LEAST 3
   Using? _____

   How can we document? (A training syllabus that specifies a course, workshop, etc., would be an example)

C. Topics
   REQUIRED: 8
   We include a total of _____

   Which of the following do we include:

   ___ 1. Definition of tutoring and tutor responsibilities
   ___ 2. Basic tutoring guidelines
   ___ 3. Techniques for successfully beginning and ending a tutor session
   ___ 4. Some basic Tuytoring Do's
   ___ 5. Some basic Tutoring Don'ts
   ___ 6. Role Modeling
   ___ 7. Setting Goals/Planning
   ___ 8. Communication Skills
   ___ 9. Active listening & paraphrasing
   ___ 10. Referral Skills
   ___ 11. Study Skills
   ___ 12. Critical Thinking Skills
   ___ 13. Compliance with the Ethics and Philosophy of the Tutor Program
   ___ 14. Modeling problem solving
   ___ 15. Other (please specify)

How can we document? (Course syllabus, training syllabus, etc.)

D. Tutor Experience: **25 hours required for each level of certification**

   How do we document experience? (Ex.: appointment sheets, time cards, etc.)

E. Tutor Selection: **Two of the criteria required.** Which of the following criteria do we use?

   ___ 1. Written approval of a content/skill instructor
   ___ 2. Endorsement of tutor trainer/supervisor.
   ___ 3. Grade of "A" or "B" in subject content being tutored.
   ___ 4. Documented experience equivalent to #3.

How can we document? (Tutor application form, recruiting letter, job description would be examples).

F. Tutor Evaluation: **Three requirements.** Which do we have in place?

   ___ 1. A formal/informal evaluation process is in place.
   ___ 2. Formal/informal evaluation occurs on a regular basis.
   ___ 3. The results of the evaluation process are made known to the tutors.

How can we document? (Examples would be an evaluation calendar, a copy of the form used, a policy statement or evaluation and/or an example of a memo communicating results to tutors)

COLLEGE READING AND LEARNING ASSOCIATION'S

APPLICATION COVER SHEET
FOR CERTIFICATION OF TUTOR PROGRAM(S)

GENERAL INFORMATION
(PLEASE TYPE OR PRINT THE FOLLOWING INFORMATION)

1. *PROGRAM LIAISON/CONTACT PERSON AND MAILING ADDRESS:*

_____

_____

_____

PHONE #: _____ FAX #: _____ E-MAIL: _____

INSTITUTION AND PROGRAM(S) TO BE CERTIFIED: _____

_____

2. *CERTIFICATION LEVELS REQUESTED* (*please check appropriate box/boxes*):

_____REGULAR/LEVEL 1 _____ADVANCED/LEVEL 2 _____MASTER/LEVEL 3

3. *APPLICATION FEE: $50.00*
Please submit a check for $50.00 payable to **"CRLA/Tutor Certification."** Attach check to this application form. Thank you.

4. *INFORMATION AND DOCUMENT CHECKLIST:*
Please complete this checklist before mailing to make sure your application is complete.

NOTE: YOU MAY APPLY FOR MORE THAN ONE LEVEL FOR A PROGRAM AT ONE TIME, BUT IF YOU ARE APPLYING FOR MORE THAN ONE PROGRAM, YOU MUST SUBMIT COMPLETE APPLICATIONS FOR EACH SEPARATELY. DO NOT SUBMIT APPLICATIONS FOR NEW LEVELS OR NEW PROGRAMS TOGETHER WITH A RECERTIFICATION APPLICATION.

____ 1. Contact Person, Institution, and Program to be certified is identified above in each copy of the application.

____ 2. Certification Levels requested are checked above.

____ 3. Check for application fee of $50 is attached to this page on the original copy of the application.

____ 4. 1–2 page narrative overview follows this page in each copy of the application.

____ 5. Verifications follows the narrative in each copy of the application.

____ 6. Labeled documentation is tabbed and cross referenced to each verification category in each copy of the application.

Mail to: Gladys R. Shaw, Coordinator, U.T. El Paso, Tutoring & Learning Ctr., 300 Main Library, El Paso, TX 79968

OVERVIEW OF THE TUTOR PROGRAM(S) TO BE CERTIFIED

Please provide an overview, one to two pages, explaining how your tutor training program(s) fulfills the requirements of the level or levels checked. The purpose of this overview is to provide the committee members with the appropriate background information necessary to certify your program(s). This overview should provide the following information: Program history, program objectives, reporting lines, sources of funding, services and students served, program location and facility, training guidelines, and how you generally conduct your training.

PROGRAM NARRATIVE

VERIFICATION FORM

Please complete a "Verification of Tutor Program(s)" **for each program** you want to be certified. For example, if you wish to have Program A certified at Levels 1 & 2, then you would complete the verification for Levels 1 & 2 for Program A's application. If you also have a Program B that you wish to have certified at Level 1, then you would complete a separate application for Program B, Level 1 that would also include a separate verification form.

Please refer to the document titled "CRLA'S REQUIREMENTS FOR CERTIFICATION OF TUTOR PROGRAMS" for a complete listing of all the LEVEL 1, 2, AND 3 requirements for each program to be certified.

The "necessary documentation" called for under each criteria consists of patterns of evidence of the what, how, and when of the training program. It could/should include any or all of the following: 1) course syllabi; 2) titles of textbooks used; 3) flyers/posters/memos; 4) sample worksheets; and 5) handouts, worksheets, etc. that can help the CRLA Tutor Certification Committee verify your program(s). The better documentation you provide the easier it will be for the committee to certify your program(s); however, brevity is appreciated due to mailing requirements, so condensed but complete documentation is requested.

VERIFICATION OF TUTOR PROGRAM(S)

INSTITUTION/PROGRAM: _____

PROGRAM LIAISON/CONTACT PERSON: _____

Please refer to the Certification Requirements to complete the verification.

A. *AMOUNT/DURATION OF TUTOR TRAINING*

    1.   List the number of hours involved in your tutor training:
          Level 1 _____ Level 2 _____ Level 3 _____
            (Hrs)   (Hrs)   (Hrs)

    2.   Extent of Compliance. Check all that apply.

          The requirements of Level 1 (10 total required) are Met_____ Exceeded _____
          The requirements of Level 2 (20 total required) are Met_____ Exceeded _____
          The requirements for Level 3 (30 total required) are Met____Exceeded_____

    3.   Documentation that will verify the fulfillment of this requirement is attached and labeled as checked below. (Example—A Training Syllabus.) Check all that apply.

          See Document/s A.3 Level 1_____ A.3 Level 2 _____ A.3 Level 3_____

B.   *MODES OF TUTOR TRAINING*

1.   List the training modes you use in your training:

Level 1	Level 2	Level 3
_____	_____	_____
_____	_____	_____
_____	_____	_____
_____	_____	_____

2.   Extent of compliance; Check all that apply. The requirements of

Level 1 (classroom/ workshop plus any two others) are

Level 2 (classroom/ workshop plus any two others) are

Level 3 (classroom/ workshop plus any two others) are

Met ___ Exceeded ___   Met___ Exceeded ___   Met___ Exceeded ___

3.   The necessary documentation to verify the above is attached and labeled as follows: Check all that apply. (A Training Syllabus is an excellent example)

See Document/s B.3 Level 1_____   B.3 Level 2 _____   B.3 Level 3_____

C.   *AREAS/TOPICS TO BE COVERED IN TUTOR TRAINING*

1.   List which topics you cover in your training:

Level 1	Level 2	Level 3
_____	_____	_____
_____	_____	_____
_____	_____	_____
_____	_____	_____
_____	_____	_____
_____	_____	_____
_____	_____	_____
_____	_____	_____
_____	_____	_____

2.   Extent of Compliance; Check all that apply. The topic requirements of

Level 1 (8 minimum) are

Level 2 (Review of Level 1 plus at least 4 additional topics) are

Level 3 (Review of Level 1 and 2 plus 4 additional topics) are

Met___ Exceeded___   Met___ Exceeded___   Met___ Exceeded___

3. The necessary documentation to verify the above is attached and labeled as follows: (Example: Training or course syllabus.) Check all that apply.

See Document/s C.3 Level 1_____ C.3 Level 2 _____ C.3 Level 3_____

D. *REQUIRED TUTORING EXPERIENCE*

1. Explain how you keep track of your tutors' actual tutoring experience.

Level 1	Level 2	Level 3
_____	_____	_____
_____	_____	_____
_____	_____	_____
_____	_____	_____

2. Extent of compliance; Check all that apply. This procedure at

Level 1	Level 2	Level 3
Meets criteria___	Meets criteria___	Meets criteria___
Exceeds criteria___	Exceeds criteria___	Exceeds criteria___

of the CRLA requirements for tracking tutoring experience.

3. The necessary documentation to verify the above is attached and labeled as checked below. Check all that apply. (Example: time logs.)

See Document/s D.3 Level 1_____ D.3 Level 2 _____ D.3 Level 3_____

E. *TUTOR SELECTION CRITERIA*

1. Explain how your tutors are selected (must meet at least two of the criteria)

Level 1	Level 2	Level 3
_____	Met at Level 1 ___	Met at Level 1___
_____		
_____		
_____		

2. Extent of compliance; Check all that apply. This selection procedure

Level 1	Level 2	Level 3
Meets criteria___	Met at Level 1 ___	Met at Level 1 ___
Exceeds criteria___		

3. The necessary documentation to verify the above is attached and labeled as checked below. (Example: job description or application form that specifies qualifications.) Check all that apply.

    See Documentation   Met at Level 1 ____   Met at Level 1 ____
    Labeled Level
    1, E.3 ____

F.   *TUTOR EVALUATION CRITERIA*

1. How are your tutors evaluated? Check all that apply.

Level 1	Level 2	Level 3
___ an evaluation is in place	___ Met at Level 1	___ Met at Level 1
___ it occurs on a regular basis		
___ results are made by known to tutors		

2. Extent of compliance: Check all that apply.

    Meets criteria ____   Met at Level 1____   Met at Level 1____
    Exceeds criteria____

3. The necessary documentation to verify the above is attached and labeled as checked below. (Examples: evaluation calendar, evaluation forms, policy statement, copy of communication of results, etc.) Check all that apply.

    See Documentation   Met at Level 1 ____   Met at Level 1 ____
    Labeled Level
    1, F.3 _____

UNIVERSITIES AND PROGRAMS CERTIFIED BY COLLEGE READING AND LEARNING ASSOCIATION (June 2000)

Name	*Program*	*City*	*State*
University of Nebraska-Kearney	Resident Tutor Program	Kearney	NE
University of Texas-El Paso	Tutoring & Learning Ctr.	El Paso	TX
University of Alaska-Anchorage	Learning Resources Ctr.	Anchorage	AK
University of New Mexico	Ctr. for Academic Program Support	Albuquerque	NM
Eastern New Mexico Univ.	Tutoring Services	Portales	NM
Fairmont State College	Tutorial Program	Fairmont	WV
Leland High School	Peer Tutor Program	San Jose	CA
Endicott College	Peer Tutor Program	Beverly	MA
Chaminade Univ. of Honolulu	Academic Achievement Program	Honolulu	HI
West Hills College	Tutorial Program	Coalinga	CA
Pfeiffer College	Learning Center	Misenheimer	NC
Yukon College	Yukon Learn Tutor Training	Yukon	Canada
Southern Alberta Institute of Technology	Learning Skills Centre	Calgary, Alberta	Canada
Chemeketa Community College	Tutoring Services	Salem	OR
Louisiana State University	Student Support Services Program	Baton Rouge	LA
Windward Community College	STARR Program	Kaneohe	HI
Kenai Peninsula College	Tutor Program	Soldotna	AK
Kenai Peninsula College-Kachemak Bay	Peer Tutor Program	Homer	AK
Casper College	Peer Tutor Program	Casper	WY
Pima Community College-East Campus	Tutoring Ctr. Tutorial Program	Tucson	AZ

Northern Essex Community College	Peer Tutor Program	Haverhill	MA
Wayne State College	Peer Tutor Program	Wayne	NE
Sonoma State University	Tutorial Program	Rohnert Park	CA
New Mexico State University	Student Support Services	Las Cruces	NM
Glendale Community College	Tutorial Program	Glendale	CA
Schreiner College	Peer Tutor Program	Kerrville	TX
University of Vermont	Learning Skills Program	Burlington	VT
Oakton Community College	Instructional Support Services	Des Plaines	IL
Ricks College	Tutoring Center	Rexburg	ID
Ricks College	Reading Lab	Rexburg	ID
Idaho State University	Developmental Mathematics	Pocatello	ID
Idaho State University	Writing Lab	Pocatello	ID
Lakeland College-Lloyd & Vemilion	Peer Tutor Program	Vermilion	Canada
Paradise Valley Community College	Learning Assistance Ctr. Tutor Training	Phoenix	AZ
Minnesota State University	Learning Ctr.	Mankato	MN
Mendocino College	Tutoring Program	Ukiah	CA
Northeast Texas Community College	Academic Skills Ctr. Tutorial Program	Mt. Pleasant	TX
University of Texas - Austin	Learning Skills Ctr. Tutorial Assistance	Austin	TX
Pacific Lutheran University	Academic Assistance	Tacoma	WA
Des Moines Area Community College	Peer Tutoring Program	Ankey	IA
California State University - Los Angeles	University Tutorial Ctr.	Los Angeles	CA
Modesto Junior College	Tutoring Program	Modesto	CA
Black Hawk College	Tutor Training Program	Moline	IL
Rock Valley College	Tutoring Program	Rockford	IL

Central Washington University	Special Services	Ellensburg	WA
Wilmington College	Peer Tutoring Program	Wilmington	OH
St. Ambrose University	Tutoring Program	Davenport	IA
Central Arizona College	Cooperative Learning Ctr.	Coolidge	AZ
University of Northern Colorado	Tutoring Program/Ctr. For Human Enrich	Greeley	CO
University of Houston	Learning Support Services	Houston	TX
Sheridan College	Advantage Tutor Program	Sheridan	WY
Kingwood College	Academic Support Ctr.	Kingwood	TX
University of Southern California - Park	Center for Academic Support	Los Angeles	CA
Morehead State University	Special Services Learning Lab	Morehead	KY
State University of New York-Plattsburgh	Writing Tutor Training Program	Plattsburgh	NY
York Technical College	Tutoring Program	Rock Hill	SC
Colorado State University	Academic Advancement Ctr.	Fort Collins	CO
Slippery Rock University	Tutorial Ctr./Academic Support Service	Slippery Rock	PA
The University of Akron/ Wayne College	Learning Support Services	Orrville	OH
College of Charleston	Center for Student Writing Lab	Charleston	SC
University of Houston	The Challenger Program	Houston	TX
Louisiana State University	Learning Assistance Ctr. Tutor Training	Baton Rouge	LA
Brigham Young University	Tutoring	Provo	UT
College of Charleston	Languages Tutoring Lab	Charleston	SC
College of Charleston	Math Lab	Charleston	SC
Austin Community College-Northridge	Northridge Tutoring Lab	Austin	TX
University of Southern Indiana	Academic Skills/Reading & English	Evansville	IN
University of Southern Indiana	Academic Skills/Math Clinic	Evansville	IN

Boise State University	Tutorial Programs	Boise	ID
Jamestown C.C.-Cattaraugus County	Peer Tutoring Program	Olean	NY
Austin Community College-Pinnacle	Parallel Studies Learning Labs	Austin	TX
Hesser College	Peer Tutoring Program	Manchester	NH
Tyler Junior College	Project Excel Peer Tutor Program	Tyler	TX
Wayne State University	Mathematics Tutoring Program	Detroit	MI
Missouri Western State College	Center for Academic Support	St. Joseph	MO
Columbia College	Disabled Student Programs & Tutoring	Sonora	CA
Columbia College	Learning Skills Ctr. Tutorial Program	Sonora	CA
St. Edward's University	Academic & Career Services -SS Ctr.	Austin	TX
Minneapolis Community College	Learning Assistance Ctr. Tutor Training	Minneapolis	MN
Wake Forest University	Learning Assistance Program Tutorial	Winston-Salem	NC
Boston College	Learning Resources/Student Athletes	Chestnut Hill	MA
Saint Xavier University	The Learning Assistance Ctr.	Chicago	IL
Harding University	Sears Learning Ctr.	Searcy	AR
University of Pittsburgh	Math Undergraduate TA & Math Tutor	Pittsburgh	PA
Weber State University	Student Support Services	Ogden	UT
Wallace Community College	Pathways	Dothan	AL
Mt. Hood Community College	Developmental Education Division	Gresham	OR
Rutgers University	Learning Resource Ctr.	New Brunswick	NJ
Suffolk University	Ballotti Learning Ctr.	Boston	MA
Cedar Valley College	Student Support Services/TRIO Prog.	Dallas	TX

King's College	Tutoring Program	Wilkes-Barre	PA
Boston College	Academic Development Ctr. Tutoring	Chestnut Hill	MA
Patrick Henry Community College	Student Support Services	Martinsville	VA
Quinnipiac College	Learning Resources Ctr.	Hamden	CT
The Citadel	The Writing Center	Charleston	SC
Bronx Community College-City Univ. NY	PASS Center	Bronx	NY
University of New Hampshire-Manchester	Tutor Training Progr. the Learning Ctr.	Manchester	NH
University of Findlay	English 490: Writing Lab Practicum	Findlay	OH
Muhlenberg College	Peer Tutoring Program	Allentown	PA
Washington State University	Peer Tutorial Program	Pullman	WA
Salt Lake Community College	Student Support Services	Salt Lake City	UT
The University of Charleston	MET 110	Charleston	WV
Weber State University	Tutoring Services	Ogden	UT
Oxnard College	Tutor Training Program	Oxnard	CA
Brigham Young University-Hawaii	Reading/Writing Ctr.	Laie	HI
Northern Arizona University	Learning Assistance Ctr.	Flagstaff	AZ
University of Pittsburgh	Learning Skills Ctr.	Pittsburgh	PA
Jackson State Community College	Academic Assistance Ctr. Tutor Program	Jackson	TN
Loyola University Chicago	Tutoring Program	Maywood	IL
University of Texas-Arlington	SOAR Cost Share Tutorial Programs	Arlington	TX
Garden City Community College	Mary Jo Williams Comprehensive Learn.	Garden City	KS
Bakersfield College	Tutoring Program	Bakersfield	CA
University of New England	Learning Assistance Ctr.	Biddeford	ME

Appalachian State University	Tutorial Services	Boone	NC
North Seattle Community College	The Loft Writing Ctr. Plus	Seattle	WA
St. Louis Community College-Florissant	Tutoring Services Program	St. Louis	MO
University of Massachusetts-Lowell	Tutoring Services	Lowell	MA
Clovis Community College	Phi Theta Kappa Peer Tutoring Prog.	Clovis	NM
St. Philips College	Educational Support Services	San Antonio	TX
The University of Arizona	Learning Center Tutor Program	Tucson	AZ
South Plains College	Peer Tutoring Program	Levelland	TX
The College of New Jersey	Math-Sci & Writ,-Rdg. Lab Tutorial Program	Trenton	NJ
Peace College	Tutor Training Program	Raleigh	NC
Northeastern Jr. College	Study Skills Student Tutor Program	Sterling	CO
Johnson County Community College	Writing Center Peer Tutors	Overland Park	KS
Bradford College	Academic Resource Ctr.	Bradford	MA
San Diego State University	Student Affairs	San Diego	CA
Miami University	Learning Assistance	Oxford	OH
Franklin University	Teaching & Learning Ctr./Tutoring	Columbus	OH
Monroe County Community College	Learning Assistance Lab Tutoring	Monroe	MI
Long Island University-Brooklyn Campus	Academic Reinforcement Ctr.	Brooklyn	NY
Seward County Community College	Academic Achievement Ctr. Tutoring	Liberal	KS
Lake Tahoe Community College	Tutor Training Program	S. Lake Tahoe	CA
Cabrillo College	Tutorial Program	Aptos	CA
The University of Akron	Dept. of Dev. Ed. - Tutorial Program	Akron	OH

Triton College	Learning Assistance Ctr.	River Grove	IL
Paine College	Tutorial & Enrichment Ctr.	Augusta	GA
Lorain County Community College	The Individualized Learning Support Ctr.	Elyria	OH
Linn-Benton Community College	Tutoring Program	Albany	OR
Middle Tennessee State University	Developmental Studies Tutoring Prog.	Murfreesboro	TN
Southwest Texas State University	Student Learning Assistance Ctr.	San Marcos	TX
State Technical Institute-Memphis	DUCKS Peer Tutoring Program	Memphis	TN
Baker College of Flint	Learning Support Ctr.	Flint	MI
University of Massachusetts-Amherst	Learning Support Services	Amherst	MA
Lesley College	Center for Academic Achievement	Cambridge	MA
Muskingum Area Technical College	Peer Tutoring Program	Zanesville	OH
Kapi'olani Community College	Holomau Center	Honolulu	HI
University of Minnesota-Duluth	Tutoring Center	Duluth	MN
Arizona State University-West	Student Support Services Program	Phoenix	AZ
Blackburn College	Tutor/SI Program	Carlinville	IL
Blackburn College	Writing Assistants Program	Carlinville	IL
Southern Illinois University-Carbondale	Tutor Training Program	Carbondale	IL
Rose State College	Peer Tutoring Program	Midwest City	OK
U.S. Coast Guard Academy	Peer Tutor Program	New London	CT
Kent State University	Academic Service Center	Kent	OH
Kent State University	Learning Development Program	Kent	OH

Harding University	Student Support Services	Searcy	AR
Rocky Mountain College	Services for Academic Success	Billings	MT
University of Northern British Columbia	Learning Skills Centre	Prince George	Canada
California State Polytechnic - Pomona	Educational Opportunity Program	Pomona	CA
Rider University	Education Enhancement Program	Lawrenceville	NJ
Augustana College	Writing Center	Sioux Falls	SD
Johnson State College	Academic Support Services	Johnson	VT
Indiana University Northwest	The Occupational Dev. Program	Gary	IN
Western Nevada Community College	Tutorial Program	Carson City	NV
Assumption College	Academic Support Ctr.	Worcester	MA
Eastern Wyoming College	Learning Center Tutor Program	Torrington	WY
St. Norbert College	Academic Mastery Program	De Pere	WI
Baltimore City Community College	Academic Development Program	Baltimore	MD
Clemson University	Student Athlete Enrichment Programs	Clemson	SC
Ohio University	Program of Supplemental Instruction	Athens	OH
Medical College of PA & Hahnemann	Student Resource Ctr.	Philadelphia	PA
Newbury College	Academic Resource Ctr.	Brookline	MA
Brookhaven College	Tutorial Services	Famers Branch	TX
North Carolina State University	Undergraduate Studies Tutorial Ctr.	Raliegh	NC
Sullivan County Community College	Ctr. for Learning Assistance	Loch Sheldrake	NY
St. Cloud State University	Academic Learning Ctr.	St. Cloud	MN
Montana State University-Bozeman	Advance By Choice	Bozeman	MT

University of Main	Onward Tutor Program	Orono	ME
Xavier University	Learning Assistance Program	Cincinnati	OH
Morehead State University	MSU Corps. An Americorps Program	Morehead	KY
Milwaukee Area Technical College	Tutoring Ctr.	Milwaukee	WI
University of Scranton	Learning Resources Ctr.	Scranton	PA
Three Rivers Community-Technical	Peer Tutoring Program	Norwich	CT
Middlesex Community-Technical College	Learning Ctr.	Middletown	CT
University of New Hampshire	Tutoring Program of the Ctr.	Durham	NH
University of Miami	Athletic Dept., Academic Support	Coral Gables	FL
North Hennepin Community College	College Learning Ctr. Peer Tutor Prog.	Brooklyn Park	MN
California State Polytechnic - Pomona	Learning Resource Ctr.	Pomona	CA
Northwest Missouri State University	Talent Dev. Ctr.	Maryville	MO
Eastern Arizona College	Aspire Program	Thatcher	AZ
California State Univ.-San Bernardino	Learning Ctr. Tutorial Program	San Bernardino	CA
Utah Valley State College	Peer Tutoring Program	Orem	UT
New Hampshire College	Learning Ctr., Tutor Training Program	Manchester	NH
University of Tampa	Academic Ctr. For Excellence	Tampa	FL
Spelman College	Learning Resources Ctr's Peer Tutor	Atlanta	GA
Utah Valley State College	Writing Center	Orem	UT
Univ of TX-Brownsville & Southmost	Learning Assistance Ctr. Training Prog.	Brownsville	TX
Rowan College of New Jersey	Tutorial Services	Glassboro	NJ

Montana State University-Northern	Student Support Services Tutorial Prog.	Havre	MT
Piedmont College	Tutorial Ctr.	Demorest	GA
El Camino Community College	Learning Resources Ctr. Tutorial Prog.	Torrance	CA
Appalachian State University	Upward Bound	Boone	NC
University of Idaho	Tutoring & Academic Assistance Ctr.	Moscow	ID
Widener University	RAS Center	Chester	PA
University of Wisconsin-Eau Claire	Academic Skills Ctr. Tutoring	Eau Claire	WI
Walla Walla College	Teaching Learning Ctr.	College Place	WA
Allegany College	Tutoring Program	Cumberland	MD
Mount Ida College	Academic Service Center	Newton Centre	MA
Utah State University	Learning & Life Skills Ctr.	Logan	UT
Shepherd College	Tutor Training Program & Writing Ctr.	Shepherdstown	WV
Central Arizona College-Aravaipa	Learning Ctr. Tutor Training Program	Winkelman	AZ
Mesa State College	Academic Services Tutoring Program	Grand Junction	CO
Delta College	Peer Mentor Program	University Ctr.	MI
Delta College	Tutoring Program	Univeristy Ctr.	MI
Baptist Bible College	Learning Ctr.	Springfield	MO
Everett Community College	Writing Center	Everett	WA
University of TX - Austin	Tutoring Program in Rdg/Writ/SS Lab	Austin	TX
Howard Community College	Learning Assistance Ctr. Tutoring	Columbia	MD
Southwest State University	Tutor Training	Marshall	MN
Itasca Community College	Academic Resource Ctr.	Grand Rapids	MN
University of TX - Austin	Student Athlete Academic Support	Austin	TX
Hampton University	Student Support Services	Hampton	VA

Bristol Community College	Tutoring and Academic Support Ctr.	Fall River	MA
Cal Poly State Univ - San Luis Obispo	Study Group Program/ Math WS Prog.	San Luis Obisp	CA
University of La Verne	Learning Enhancement Center	La Verne	CA
New Mexico State University-Alamogordo	Math Learning Ctr.	Alamogordo	NM
Northern Illinois University	ACCESS/Peer Assisted Learning	DeKalb	IL
Woodbury University	Learning Ctr.	Burbank	CA
Ft. Lewis College	Program for Academic Advancement	Durango	CO
Abilene Christian University	Learning Enhancement Ctr.	Abilene	TX
University of Bridgeport	Academic Resource Ctr.	Bridgeport	CT
Columbus State University	Tutorial Services Program	Columbus	GA
Virginia Tech	The Ctr for Academic Enrichment & Exc	Blacksburg	VA
Amarillo College	Peer Tutoring	Amarillo	TX
Evergreen Valley College	Tutoring Program	San Jose	CA
Creighton University	Tutor Training Program	Omaha	NE
Southwestern Oregon Community College	Tutoring Lab	Coos Bay	OR
University of NM - Valencia Campus	Learning & Resource Ctr.	Los Lunas	NM
Lake Superior College	Learning Resource Ctr.	Duluth	MN
Loyola College	Peer Tutoring Program	Baltimore	MD
University of the Pacific	Supportive Services Program	Stockton	CA
Bryant College	Tutor Training Program	Smithfield	RI
Ivy Tech State College	The Learning Ctr. Tutoring Program	Ft. Wayne	IN
Laramie County Community College	Student Success Ctr./ System for SS	Cheyenne	WY
Harford Community College	Tutoring Program	Bel Air	MD

Cochise College	Campus Wide Tutoring Program	Douglas	AZ
Randolph Macon College	Patrick John Higgins Academic Ctr.	Ashland	VA
Tennessee Technological University	Academic Dev. Learning Ctr.	Cookeville	TN
Wellesley College	Tutor Program	Wellesley	MA
Wellesley College	Peer Tutor Advisor/Peer Tutor Assoc.	Wellesley	MA
Florida Atlantic University	Tutorial Assistance Program	Boca Raton	FL
Santa Barbara City College	Tutorial 199	Santa Barbara	CA
Durham Technical Community College	Campus Learning Center	Durham	NC
Saint Anselm College	Academic Resource Ctr. Peer Tutor	Manchester	NH
State University of NY (SUNY)	Agriculture & Technology at Morrisville	Morrisville	NY
Shelby State Community College	Learning Assistance Ctr.	Memphis	TN
Arizona State University	Student Affairs Learning Resource Ctr.	Tempe	AZ
Lake Superior State University	Learning Ctr. Tutor Program	Sault Ste. Marie	MI
Massasoit Community College	Academic Resource Ctr.	Brockton	MA
Hawaii Community College	The Learning Ctr., Tutor Training Prog.	Hilo	HI
Central Arizona College	Tutor Training Program	Apache Junctio	AZ
St. Thomas Aquinas	Academic Skills Ctr.	Sparkill	NY
Cloud County Community College	Peer Tutor Program	Concordia	KS
Capital Community-Tech College	Math Ctr.	Hartford	CT
Idaho State University	ASISU Content Area Tutoring	Pocatello	ID
McMurry University	Academic Enrichment Ctr.	Abilene	TX

Holyoke Community College	Learning Assistance Ctr.	Holyoke	MA
Las Positas College	Tutorial Program	Livermore	CA
Portland Community College	Tutor for Credit Program	Portland	OR
Tarleton State University	Teaching Learning Ctr. Tutor Training	Stephenville	TX
Kankakee Community College	Academic Skills Ctr.	Kankakee	IL
Lincoln Land Community College	Tutoring Services	Springfield	IL
Cayuga Community College	Academic Support Center	Auburn	NY
Shippensburg University	Learning Assistance Ctr.	Shippensburg	PA
University of Connecticut	Ctr. for Academic Programs, SSS	Storrs	CT
University of Pittsburgh-Bradford	Academic Dev. Ctr.-Tutoring Program	Bradford	PA
New Hampshire Tech. Community College	Learning & Career Ctr: Peer Tutor Prog.	Stratham	NH
Mt. San Antonio College	Tutorial Services	Walnut	CA
San Jose State University	Collaborative Training Institute	San Jose	CA
Glendale Community College	Learning Assistance Ctr. Tutor Training	Glendale	AZ
Abilene Christian University	Alph Academic Service	Abilene	TX
Univ. of Nevada - Reno	The Academic Skills Center	Reno	NV
Waldorf College	Academic Achievement Ctr. Tutoring	Forest City	IA
Duluth Business Univ.	Student Mentoring Program	Duluth	MN
Heartland Community College	Tutor Program	Bloomington	IL
University of Southern Colorado	Student Support Services	Pueblo	CO
University of North Florida	Academic Resource Center	Jacksonville	FL
Pacific University	Tutorial Center	Stockton	CA

Pacific University	Language Arts	Stockton	CA
Pacific University	Mathematics Resource Ctr.	Stockton	CA
Gaston College	Peer Tutoring Program	Dallas	NC
Utah Valley State College	ATAC Assisted Learning Program	Orem	UT
Lake Michigan College	Transitional Studies Tutoring Program	Benton Harbor	MI
Bucks County Community College	ACT 101 - Goals Program	Newtown	PA
Univ. of College of the Cariboo	Writing Ctr.	Kamloops	Canada
Charleston Southern University	The Learning Center	Charleston	SC
Rockhurst College	Learning Ctr. Tutor Training Program	Kansas City	MO
Beaver College	Education Enhancement Ctr.	Glenside	PA
Phoenix College	Learning Ct. Tutor Training Program	Phoenix	AZ
The C.C. of Baltimore County Essex Camp	Tutoring Program	Baltimore	MD
Univ. of California-Irvine	Learning & Academic Resource Ctr.	Irvine	CA
Arizona State University	Writing Center	Tempe	AZ
Becker College	Academic Support Services	Worcester	MA
Wayne State College	STRIDE Student Support Services	Wayne	NE
Ranken Technical College	Tutor Training Program	St. Louis	MO
Kettering University	Tutor Program	Flint	MI
Albuquerque Tech.-Vocational Institute	Assistance Ctrs for Education	Albuquerque	NM
MidSouth Community College	Learning Center	West Memphis	AR
Bryant & Stratton College	Tutor Program	Cleveland	OH
Texas A & M-Corpus Christi	Tutoring & Learning Ctr.	Corpus Christi	TX
Allan Hancock College	Tutorial Ctr.	Santa Maria	CA

Schreiner College	Learning Support Services	Kerrville	TX
Oakland University	Academic Skills Ctr.	Rochester	MI
Weatherford College	Success Connection	Weatherford	TX
Hiwassee College	Student Support Services	Madisonville	TN
Philadelphia University	The Academic Science Center	Philadelphia	PA
Community College of Rhode Island	Access to Opportunity Program	Warwick	RI
Massachusetts Bay Community College	Peer Tutoring Program	Wellesley Hills	MA
Northwest College	Peer Tutor Program	Powell	WY
TX A & M International University	The AEC Tutoring Ctr.	Laredo	TX
Lehigh Carbon Community College	Writing Lab	Schnecksville	PA
Dyersburg State Community College	Student Success Ctr.	Dyersburg	TN
El Paso Community College	Ctr. for Students with Disabilities	El Paso	TX
Biola University	Learning Assistance Services	La Mirada	CA
University of Vermont	Subject-Area Tutoring Program	Burlington	VT
Kutztown University	Tutoring Program	Kutztown	PA
Lansing Community College	Tutorial Services	Lansing	MI
Purdue University-North Central	Student Support Services	Westville	IN
U.T. Pan American	Learning Assistance Ctr. Tutoring Prog.	Edinburg	TX
Northampton Community College	Learning Center	Bethlehem	PA
Sault College	Peer Tutor Program	Marie ON	Canada
Loyola Marymount University	Learning Resource Ctr.	Los Angeles	CA
SUNY at Buffalo	Educ. Opportunity Prog. Tutorial Comp.	Buffalo	NY

Harrisburg Area Community College	Writing Lab Tutor Training	Harrisburg	PA
Alfred State College	Peer Tutoring Program	Alfred	NY
Union County College	Academic Learning Centers	Cranford	NJ
El Paso Community College	Tutorial Services	El Paso	TX
Arizona State University	Freshman Year Exp. Tutoring Program	Tempe	AZ
Lakeland Community College	Tutorial Services	Kirtland	OH
Western Nebraska Community College	Tutor Program	Scottsbluff	NE
Santiago Canyon College	Tutoring Ctr.-Tutor Training Program	Orange	CA
Chattanooga State Tech Community College	Mathematics Ctr.	Chattanooga	TN
Mount Wachusett Community College	Writing Center	Gardner	MA
Chabot College	Tutorials Instructional Program	Hayward	CA
Lane Community College	Tutor Program	Eugene	OR
University of Pennsylvania	Tutoring & Learning Resources	Philadelphia	PA
Eastern Oklahoma State College	Student Support Services	Wilburton	OK
McLennan Community College	Student Support Services	Waco	TX
Kent State Trumbull Campus	Skill Center	Warren	OH
Montgomery County Community College	Learning Assistance Lab	Blue Bell	PA
The Bell Foundation	Bell Foundation	Cambridge	MA
Colorado College	Peer Tutoring in Writing Program	Colorado Springs	CO
St. Louis Community College-Meramec	Peer Tutoring Program	St. Louis	MO
Grace College	Tutoring Program	Winona Lake	IN

Anna Maria College	Learning Center	Paxton	MA
University of Wisconsin-Waukesha	Study Ctr. Tutoring Program	Waukesha	WI
Humboldt State University	Learning Center	Arcata	CA
Sunshine Coast University	Peer Advisor Training	Queensland	Australia
Cincinnati State Tech & Community College	Tutoring Centers Program	Cincinnati	OH
Bunker Hill Community College	The Success Program	Boston	MA
Central Wyoming College	Student Support Services	Riverton	WY
Holy Cross College	Learning Resource Center	Nortre Dame	IN
New Hampshire Community Tech College	Peer Tutor Program	Manchester	NH
Pioneer High School	Peer Tutor Program	San Jose	CA
SUNY-Cortland	Academic Support & Achievement Pro	Cortland	NY
Trinity College	Academic Resource Center	Washington	DC
Saint Francis	Learning Resource Ctr. Tutorial Prog.	Loretto	PA
West Chester University	University Tutoring Center	West Chester	PA
Hazard Community College	Student Support Serv. Tutoring Prog.	Hazard	KY
DeVry Institute of Technology-Dupage	Academic Support Center	Addison	IL
The Univ. of Maryland Baltimore County	The Learning Resources Ct & SSS	Baltimore	MD
University of Southern California	Student Athlete Acad. Serv. Tutoring	Los Angeles	CA
Lycoming College	Writing Tutor Training Program	Williamsport	PA
Tomball College	Learning Assistance Ctr. Tutor Dev. Prog.	Tomball	TX
Univ. of Central Arkansas	University of Writing Center	Conway	AR
Univ. of Wyoming	Academic Services	Laramie	WY
Wayne State University	Academic Dev. Services Tutorial ... Ctr.	Detroit	MI

Providence College	Tutorial Center	Providence	RI
Central Piedmont Community College	Academic Learning Ctr. T.T. Program	Charlotte	NC
College of the Redwoods	Tutor Training Program	Eureka	CA
CUPA Venango Campus	Learning Support Ctr.	Oil City	PA
North Harris College	Learning Ctr. Tutor Program	Houston	TX
College of St. Mary	Tutor Training Program	Omaha	NE
Eastern Washington University	Academic Support Center	Cheney	WA
Texas State Technical College	Dept. of Dev. Studies	Harlingen	TX
Randolph-Macon Woman's College	PASS Study Skills Tutoring Prog.	Lynchburg	VA
Wichita State University	Student Support Services	Wichita	KS
University of Puerto Rico	Dev. Education Program	Utuado	PR
University of Maryland-College Park	Academic Achievement Program	College Park	MD
University of New South Wales	Writing Assistant Program	Sydney	NSWale
University of Maryland	Academic Support & Career Dev	College Park	MD
NYACK	College Tutor Training Program	Nyack	NY
Worchester Polytechnic Institute	Academic Resource Center	Worchester	MA
City College of San Francisco	Tutor Training Program	San Francisco	CA
Shawnee State University	Student Success Center	Portsmouth	OH
Western Wyoming Community College	Peer Tutor Center	Rock Springs	WY
St. Louis Community College-Meramec	SI Program	Kirkwood	MO
Northwest Arkansas Community College	Tutor Program	Bentonville	AR
North Bend High School	Tutor Program	North Bend	OR

Crestwood High School	MuAlpha Theta Tutoring Program	Sumter	SC
College of Staten Island/CUNY	Learning Assistance Resource Ctr.	Staten Island	NY
Bowdoin College	The Quantitative Skills Program	Brunswick	ME
Ferris State University	Academic Support Center	Big Rapids	MI
Sonoma State University	Pre College Program	Rohnert Park	CA
John A Logan College	Student Success Center	Carterville	IL
Sam Houston State University	Academic Enrichment Ctr.	Huntsville	TX
Bismarck State College	Peer Tutoring Program	Bismarck	ND
Univ. of Puerto Rico at Bayamon	Tutoirng Program of the Biology Dept.	Bayamon	PR
University of Georgia	Tutorial Program	Athens	GA
York University	Learning Disabilities Program	North York	Ont.
Southern Utah University	Learning Ctr/Tutoring & Testing	Cedar City	UT
Cedar Crest College	The Advising Ctrs. Tutor Training Prog	Allentown	PA
Taylor University	Learning Support Center	Ft. Wayne	IN
Mount Royal College	Learning Skills Centre	Calgary Albert	Canada
Univ. of Northern British Columbia	Learning Skills Centre-Math T.Pro	Prince Georg	Canada
Kean University	EEP Learning Assistance	Union	NJ
Madonna University	Tutor Program	Livonia	MI
North Hennepin Community College	Peer Tutor Program	Brooklyn Park	MN
Highline Community College	Tutoring Center	Des Moines	WA
Atlantic Cape Community College	Tutor Certif. Program	Mays Landing	NJ
Pennsylvania College of Technology	Tutoring Center	Williamsport	PA
Texas Tech University	TECHniques Center	Lubbock	TX

Ozarks Technical Community College	Academic Achievement Center T.P.	Springfield	MO
Purdue University-West Lafayette	HORIZONS Student Support Program	West Lafayette	IN
Univ. of Missouri-Rolla	Writing Across the Curr. Tut T. Prog.	Rolla	MO
Nashville State Tech Institute	Education 1000	Nashville	TN
Frostburg State University	LA Ctr. Tutoring Program	Frostburg	MD
Frostburg State University	Writing Center Tutoring Program	Frostburg	MD
United State Military Academy	CEP Co. & Tutor Program	West Point	NY
S.W. Virginia College & Tech. College	Tutor Educ. Support Team Prog.	Mount Gay	WV
North Lake College	SSS Trio Program	Irving	TX
Centenary College	Academic Support Ctr. Tutorial Prog.	Hackettstown	NJ
Adrian College	Office of Academic Service Peer T.P.	Adrian	MI
Kirtland Community College	Tutorial Program	Roscommon	MI
University of Kansas	Supportive Educ. Services	Lawrence	KS

UNM Library
Instruction Tutor
Program Documents

LIBRARY INSTRUCTION SURVEY –
SPRING 1996

Dear CAPS Patron:

In the Fall of 1996, CAPS will begin tutoring Library Instruction. Please assist us in developing the program content by taking the time to complete this brief survey.

Your participation is greatly appreciated.

Which of the following library services have you used in addition to CAPS?

__Reference Department   __Copy Center
__Circulation   __Government Information
__Reserves   __Center for Southwest Research
__Interlibrary loan

Which of the following would you be interested in learning more about? Please check all that apply.

Overview of Zimmerman and Services Available:

__Reference Department   __Copy Center
__Circulation   __Government Information
__Interlibrary Loan   __Center for Southwest Research

Appendix B reprinted with permission from the University of New Mexico.

LIBROS, On-line catalog:

    __Search Strategies (Narrow or broaden topics)
    __How to locate Call Numbers and Locations
    __How to find Books
    __How to find Journal Titles
    __How to find Journal Articles

INTERNET:

    __FirstSearch Database (Access to books, articles, and newspapers.)
    __Remote Access to LIBROS and other services
    __UNM General Libraries Home Page

Could you please indicate how often you use the following services?

How often do you use LIBROS?
    __Never   __Monthly
    __At least once per week   __2 or 3 times a semester
    __2 or 3 times a week

How often do you use EBSCOhost Academic FullTEXT Elite?
    __Never   __Monthly
    __At least once per week   __2 or 3 times a semester
    __2 or 3 times a week

How often do you use Uncover?
    __Never   __Monthly
    __At least once per week   __2 or 3 times a semester
    __2 or 3 times a week

How often do you access LIBROS remotely?
    __Never   __Monthly
    __At least once per week   __2 or 3 times a semester
    __2 or 3 times a week

Have you used CD-ROM products in the Zimmerman Library?
    __Never   __Monthly
    __At least once per week   __2 or 3 times a semester
    __2 or 3 times a week

During the past year would library strategies tutoring have been helpful?
    __Yes   __No

Once this service is available, how likely are you to use this resource?
    __Not at all Likely   __Somewhat Likely   __Very Likely

Comments:

Thank you for your assistance.

LIBRARY STRATEGIES TUTORS NEEDED AT CAPS

APPLY NOW FOR JOB IN THE FALL!

JOB DESCRIPTION: Apply for a newly developed program to help students one-on-one with Library related needs. Library Strategies Tutors will assist students on how to use LIBROS, FirstSearch, and Web navigation. They will also tutor search strategies, vocabulary, and Boolean searching methods on all databases.

The job will require 15 to 20 hours a week. Hours are determined by CAPS and are Monday through Thursday 9–7, Friday 9–2, and Saturday 11–4. Weekly meetings are held from 2–5 on Fridays and are mandatory for all employees. In-depth tutor training will begin the Wednesday before classes start and will last two and a half days. You will be paid for all meetings, training sessions, breakfasts, and lunches. Library content training will begin the first week of classes and will continue until the third week of classes when you will begin to tutor Library Strategies.

CAPS will be hiring 3 to 4 people to cover 65 hours per week. Work study qualified applications are preferred but are not required. The hourly pay for undergraduates starts at $5.65 and graduate students start at $6.15. In January 1997, CAPS will be offering a Graduate Assistantship to the Library Strategies Team Leader who will oversee the program. The Library Strategies Team Leader will receive a full tuition waiver and a monthly stipend.

If you are interested, please fill out an application at CAPS (located on the third floor of Zimmerman Library). On the application you will be asked to fill in an area you would like to tutor. Write in Library Strategies as your subject area.

UNIVERSITY OF NEW MEXICO
GENERAL TUTOR EMPLOYMENT APPLICATION

WORKSTUDY

Date: _____

Number of hours desired each week: _____

Application for:

Fall   Spring   Summer

GENERAL INFORMATION

E-Mail _____

Name _____ SSN _____ Phone _____

Present Address _____ Additional Phone _____

_____ ZIP Code _____

*please inform us of any change to your address or phone #

Academic Major _____ Minor _____ College _____

Enrolled in _____ hours (for semester you are requesting employment)

Expected Semester/Year of Graduation _____

Will you be concurrently employed at another job?   **YES**   **NO**

EXPERIENCE/EXPERTISE

Describe any previous tutoring experience: _____

_____

Supervisor (name/phone): _____

Related Work Experience — Please list any work experience that will enhance your tutorial skills. (You may attach a resume if you desire).

_____

_____

_____

Indicate primary subject you wish to tutor: _____

List any other subjects you would be willing to tutor: _____

List specific course numbers on back.

Provide two references including at least one professor (name, address, phone) and one letter of reference from a professor. (Please attach it to application).

1. _____

_____

2. _____

_____

Please attach an unofficial transcript to this application.

Signature: _____ Date: _____

UNIVERSITY OF NEW MEXICO
GENERAL TUTOR EMPLOYMENT APPLICATION

NON-WORKSTUDY

Date: _____

Number of hours desired each week: _____

Application for:

Fall   Spring   Summer

GENERAL INFORMATION

E-Mail _____

Name _____ SSN _____ Phone _____

Present Address _____ Additional Phone _____

_____ ZIP Code _____

*please inform us of any change to your address or phone #

Academic Major _____ Minor _____ College _____

Enrolled in _____ hours (for semester you are requesting employment)

Expected Semester/Year of Graduation _____

Will you be concurrently employed at another job?   **YES**   **NO**

EXPERIENCE/EXPERTISE

Describe any previous tutoring experience: _____

_____

Supervisor (name/phone): _____

Related Work Experience — Please list any work experience that will enhance your tutorial skills. (You may attach a resume if you desire).

_____

_____

_____

Indicate primary subject you wish to tutor: _____

List any other subjects you would be willing to tutor: _____

List specific course numbers on back.

Provide two references including at least one professor (name, address, phone) and one letter of reference from a professor. (Please attach it to application).

1. _____

_____

2. _____

_____

Please attach an unofficial transcript to this application.

Signature: _____ Date: _____

CENTER FOR ACADEMIC PROGRAM SUPPORT (CAPS)
TUTOR INTERVIEW

Applicant:_____ Date:_____

Topics Discussed:

☐ Job Duties and Expectations (Review Duties and Responsibilities List)

☐ CAPS Services

☐ Salary and CRLA certification

☐ Evaluations

☐ Description of organization

☐ CAPS Philosophy

☐ Training

☐ Scheduling

Questions:

1. Briefly describe your previous work history, particularly involving tutoring and/or instructing.

2. Why are you interested in being a tutor with CAPS?

3a. If you have tutored previously, what did you learn from the experience?

3b. If you have not tutored, what have you learned from an employment situation?

4. Describe the most challenging situation in either area and how you handled it.

5. If you have ever received tutoring, please talk about the experience.

6. How would you describe the difference between tutoring and instructing?

7. If hired, what do you think will make you an effective tutor?

8. Please describe yourself as a student.

9. Please talk about any experience you have had working with individuals from different cultures or socio-economic backgrounds.

10. What types of people do you get along with best?

11. What type of people do you have difficulty getting along with?

12. How do you manage to get along with these people?

13. What are your organizational strategies?

14. Please describe your relationship with your instructors and your department.

15. What do you consider one of your most valuable strengths.

16. What one characteristic, either professional or personal, would you like to work on?

CENTER FOR ACADEMIC PROGRAM SUPPORT (CAPS)
TEAM LEADER INTERVIEW

Applicant:_____ Date:_____

Topics Discussed:

☐ Job Duties and Expectations (Review   ☐ Evaluations
Duties and Responsibilities List)
                                         ☐ Training Responsibilities

☐ CAPS Services   ☐ Scheduling Responsibilities

☐ Salary and GA contract

Questions:

1. Briefly describe your previous work history, including tutoring and/or instructing.

2. Why are you interested in being a tutor team leader and what would you expect from such a position?

3. What do you think it means to be a team leader versus a supervisor?

4. What qualities do you think are important to being a successful team leader?

5. What is your previous experience leading a group, or coordinating a project?

6. What strategies have you used to be a successful student?

7. Please describe your relationships with your instructors and your department(s).

8. Have you ever functioned as a liaison between different groups?

9. What experience, if any, have you had working with individuals from other cultures, or different social orientations? What did you find frustrating, rewarding?

10. How would you describe yourself as a leader?

11. How do you function most effectively?

    Under close supervision?

    Independently?

12. What do you consider one of your most valuable strengths?

13. What one characteristic, either professional or personal, do you feel you need to work on?

14. For current tutors:

    A. Given your experience at CAPS, what ideas do you have regarding the development of the _____ Team?

    B. How would you go about developing good working relationships with CAPS staff? With CAPS tutors?

15. For new applicants:

    A. What ideas do you have for fostering team development?

    B. How would you go about developing good working relationships with CAPS staff? With CAPS tutors?

The following "what if" type questions have no correct answers.

1. Suppose you have a tutor working 10 hours per week with a 2 percent utilization rate. What ideas would you have to improve the utilization rate?

2. If you were hiring a tutor, what characteristics would you be looking for?

3. What ideas do you have for working with a tutor who regularly comes late to work?

4. What questions do you have?

Library Instruction Team Leader Duties and Responsibilities
Participation in Team Leader Group
Attends regular meetings of Team Leaders
Provides information and feedback from tutors in content group
Provides information and feedback from Library Instruction Tutor Coordinator
Writes reports on a monthly and end-of-semester basis

Coordination of Activities within the Content Team
Communicates goals of the Management Team to content team
Plans group activities such as weekly tutor meetings, workshops, test reviews
Detects and handles problems within the group
Responsible for coordinating scheduling with Operations Team
Provides tutoring in the content area
Coordinates development of instructional materials
Coordinates continuous development of curriculum guides in the content area

Participation in Recruiting, Hiring, and Training of Tutors
Recruits and hires tutors in collaboration with Program Manager and LITC
    Reviews applications (courses taken, grades, recommendations)
    Checks references if appropriate
    Participates in tutor interviews (assesses communication skills, ability to work
        with other team members) as needed
Participates in training and evaluation of tutors
    Holds weekly meetings
    Explains procedures
    Acts as a role model
    Provides supervision/feedback during tutor probationary period
    Participates in evaluation process
    Provides content expertise to work group

Serves as CAPS Liaison with Library Instruction Tutor Coordinator
Establishes and maintains contact with LITC
Collects course syllabi and samples of special assignments
Communicates CAPS services to LITC and library personnel
Makes classroom visits to promote Library Instruction services
Establishes routine communication process (e.g., e-mail, mailbox, regular meetings,
    etc.) with LITC and other library personnel

Required Abilities
Content expertise in specialized subject are as demonstrated by high grades or work
    experience; and enrollment in a graduate program and/or faculty
    recommendation
Good communication, organizational, and interpersonal skills

Establishes Working Relationship with CAPS Management Team Contact
Consults for problem-solving assistance
Maintains regular communication—meetings, reports, etc.
Reports personnel problems
Establishes priorities and objectives for each semester

Name: _____   Workgroup: _____

TIME	MON	TUES	WED	THUR	FRI	SAT	SUN
8:00							
:30							
9:00							
:30							
10:00							
:30							
11:00							C
:30							
12:00							L
:30							
1:00							O
:30							
2:00							S
:30							
3:00							E
:30							
4:00							D
:30							
5:00							
:30							
6:00							
:30							
TOTAL							

CAPS hours are: Monday thru Thursday............................9 am – 7 pm

Friday..9 am – 2 pm

Saturday..11 am – 4 pm

UNIVERSITY OF NEW MEXICO GENERAL LIBRARY
EDUCATION PROGRAMS AND SERVICES

CENTER FOR ACADEMIC PROGRAM SUPPORT—CAPS

Welcome to the Center for Academic Program Support—CAPS! CAPS is a free-of-charge educational assistance program available to UNM students.

The tutors at CAPS are UNM upper-class undergraduates and graduate students. The CAPS tutor-training program is certified by a national college association.

REGISTRATION

To receive services at CAPS, please register in person with a CAPS receptionist on the third floor of Zimmerman Library. A current LOBO ID card is required.

ONE-ON-ONE TUTORING

A student may have up to 100 minutes of tutoring per course, per week for most undergraduate courses. A student must be officially enrolled in the course for which tutoring is requested.

In addition to tutoring specific undergraduate courses, CAPS also tutors library research and study strategies.

Making Appointments: One-on-one tutoring appointments may be made in person at CAPS or by phoning 277-4560. Appointments may be made one week in advance.

WALK-IN LABS

Tutors are available in the walk-in labs to assist students with questions related to course work. Appointments are not required. Walk-in labs are available in the following areas:

- Algebra Lab • Trigonometry/Calculus Lab • Writing Lab
- Chemistry Lab • Physics Lab

GROUP INSTRUCTION

Tutors conduct weekly language conversation groups, including Spanish, French, Italian, and German. Tutors also conduct topic-specific workshops and reviews for various subjects throughout the semester.

LOCATION

CAPS is located on the third floor of Zimmerman Library. One-on-one tutoring and all but one of the walk-in labs are held at this location. The Calculus walk-in lab is held at Centennial Science and Engineering Library.

LEARNING SUPPORT SERVICES (LSS)

Education Programs and Services offers a program for students with learning disabilities. Additional information about this program is available from CAPS receptionists or from the LSS office. Please stop by or call 277-8291.

Registrar's Initials _____

CAPS STUDENT REGISTRATION CARD

| | | |

Student ID/Social Security Number   Phone Number

Last

First   MI   @unm.edu

e-mail

1. Is this the first time you have registered with CAPS?   Yes   No
2. If an undergraduate, are you a first-semester freshman?   Yes   No
3. Please check **one**:

    ☐ Undergraduate   ☐ Graduate   ☐ Non-Degree

4. Please check the **one** college in which you are enrolled:

    ☐ Architecture   ☐ Arts & Sciences   ☐ BUS
    ☐ Business   ☐ Education   ☐ Engineering
    ☐ Fine Arts   ☐ Health Science Colleges   ☐ Undergraduate Studies
    ☐ Other

5. For how many hours are you enrolled? _____

DO NOT WRITE BELOW THIS LINE

For Tutor Only

Explain CAPS Services
    ☐ Scheduled Appointments   ☐ Drop-In Labs   ☐ Instructor Notification

Explain Student Responsibilities
    ☐ Be on Time   ☐ No Show Policy
    ☐ Be Prepared   ☐ Follow Library Policy on Food and Drink
    ☐ Making Appointments   ☐ Participate in Tutor Evaluations
    ☐ Canceling Appointments

Explain Tutoring Process
    ☐ Questioning   ☐ Summarizing

Tutor Name: _____

CAPS LIBRARY INSTRUCTION
USER SURVEY

1. How often did you use a library in your studies before you came to UNM?

    A) Not at all   B) 1 to 3 times a month
    C) 4 to 6 times a month   D) More than 6 times a month

2. Have you used other large academic libraries before? _____ Yes _____ No

3. Please indicate the type of use you have made of UNM libraries prior to this tutoring session.

    __ LIBROS on-line catalog   __ Copy Services   __Expanded Academic Index
    __ Circulation   __ UnCover   __Reserves
    __ FirstSearch   __ Reference

4. Please check off the instructional sessions you have attended at UNM General Library.

    __ Navigating LIBROS   __ Surfing LIBROS   __Exploring FirstSearch

5. Can you define the Boolean Operators and how they effect a search?

    AND   **OR**   **NOT**

6. Have you ever asked for assistance at the reference desk? __ Yes __ No

7. My previous library training includes:
    (Check as many of these as seem appropriate to your situation.)

    ___a) How to use a card catalog

    ___b) How to use reference books (encyclopedias, dictionaries, etc.)

    ___c) How to use *Readers' Guide to Periodical Literature*

    ___d) How to use the Dewey Decimal System

    ___e) How to use the Library of Congress Classification System

    ___f) How to use periodical indexes (other than *Readers' Guide*)

    ___g) How to use an on-line catalog

    ___h) How to use the Internet

    ___i) How to use CD-ROM indexes

TUTORING SERVICES EVALUATION

In order that CAPS may continue to provide high quality service to you, the student, we like to periodically solicit your input. Please take a few minutes to complete this evaluation form. The information you provide will be used to recognize outstanding service providers and to aid the CAPS Management Team in identifying areas needing improvement.

Thank you for taking the time to complete this evaluation.

Please use a separate form for each tutor being evaluated.

Tutor's Name:

_____

Subject:

_____

Course #:

_____

Is this the first time that you've met with this tutor?
[ ] Yes [ ] No

This tutor is friendly and eager to help
[ ] Strongly Agree [ ] Agree [ ] Disagree [ ] Strongly Disagree

This tutor is on time
[ ] Strongly Agree [ ] Agree [ ] Disagree [ ] Strongly Disagree

This tutor is prepared
[ ] Strongly Agree [ ] Agree [ ] Disagree [ ] Strongly Disagree

I am comfortable asking this tutor questions
[ ] Strongly Agree [ ] Agree [ ] Disagree [ ] Strongly Disagree

This tutor appears to know the material being covered
[ ] Strongly Agree [ ] Agree [ ] Disagree [ ] Strongly Disagree

This tutor helps me to understand the material by using good examples
[ ] Strongly Agree [ ] Agree [ ] Disagree [ ] Strongly Disagree

After meeting with this tutor, I am able to continue the work on my own
[ ] Strongly Agree [ ] Agree [ ] Disagree [ ] Strongly Disagree

This tutor expects me to do most of the work rather than doing the work for me
[ ] Strongly Agree [ ] Agree [ ] Disagree [ ] Strongly Disagree

This tutor helps me to understand the general concepts of the material
[ ] Strongly Agree [ ] Agree [ ] Disagree [ ] Strongly Disagree

This tutor is patient and waits for me to give my answers
[ ] Strongly Agree [ ] Agree [ ] Disagree [ ] Strongly Disagree

This tutor listens to my questions and understands my needs
[ ] Strongly Agree [ ] Agree [ ] Disagree [ ] Strongly Disagree

This tutor asks questions to help me identify what I know and don't know
[ ] Strongly Agree [ ] Agree [ ] Disagree [ ] Strongly Disagree

This tutor helps me to summarize what I have learned during the tutoring session
[ ] Strongly Agree [ ] Agree [ ] Disagree [ ] Strongly Disagree

Would you like to work with this tutor again?
[ ] Yes [ ] No

Comments:

Please return this form to the CAPS Receptionist.

Thanks again for taking the time to complete this evaluation.

TENTS POSTED ON TERMINALS IN REFERENCE AREA

DO YOU WANT TO BE
A MORE EXPERT LIBRARY USER?

The "Library Instruction" Tutors at the Center for Academic Program Support (CAPS) can help!

The service offers one-on-one appointments for beginning library research assistance. Fellow students trained in library strategies will assist you with focusing a topic, analyzing a search strategy, and finding books, articles, and other research materials. You will learn about electronic resources such as LIBROS, UnCover, EBSCOHost, and over 64 databases available through FirstSearch.

Make appointments at CAPS, located on the third floor of Zimmerman Library. CAPS hours are:

Monday–Thursday	9:00 am to 7:00 pm
Friday	9:00 am to 2:00 pm
Saturday	11:00 am to 4:00 pm

Services are available to ALL UNM students.

Appendix C

UNM Library Instruction Tutor Program Training Agenda and Exercises

FALL 1996 – CAPS NEW TUTOR TRAINING AGENDA

Wednesday, August 21st

1:00 p.m.–1:25 p.m.	Introduction by CAPS Director
1:25 p.m.–2:15 p.m.	Tour of CAPS
2:15 p.m.–2:30 p.m.	Break
2:30 p.m.–4:15 p.m.	Overview of CAPS (Part I)
4:15 p.m.–4:30 p.m.	Review and Wrap-up

Thursday, August 22nd

8:00 a.m.–8:35 a.m.	Breakfast
8:40 a.m.–9:45 a.m.	Overview of CAPS (Part II)
9:45 a.m.–10:00 a.m.	Break
10:00 a.m.–11:50 a.m.	Overview of Tutoring (Mock Tutoring)
12:00 p.m.–1:00 p.m.	Lunch
1:10 p.m.–1:40 p.m.	CAPS Director, Welcome
1:40 p.m.–4:00 p.m.	Scheduling and Team Meetings

Friday, August 23rd

8:00 a.m.–8:35 a.m.	Breakfast
8:40 a.m.–9:10 a.m.	Ethics
9:10 a.m.–9:45 a.m.	Boundaries
9:45 a.m.–10:00 a.m.	Break
10:00 a.m.–10:15 a.m.	Referrals
10:15 a.m.–11:50 a.m.	Students with Learning Disabilities
12:00 a.m.–1:00 p.m.	Lunch
1:10 p.m.–2:10 p.m.	Grab Bag Review
2:10 p.m.–2:20 p.m.	Break
2:20 p.m.–2:35 p.m.	Standards
2:35 p.m.–3:20 p.m.	Questions & Answers
3:20 p.m.–3:30 p.m.	Break
3:30 p.m.–4:00 p.m.	New Programs
4:00 p.m.–4:15 p.m.	Wrap-up

FALL 1996-LIBRARY INSTRUCTION TUTOR TRAINING AGENDA

Tuesday, August 27th

3:15 p.m.–5:15 p.m.   Session 1: Introduction to Campus Libraries

7:00 p.m.–9:00 p.m.   Session 2: Windows® 95, Internet Browsers and Computer Accounts

Thursday, August 29th

3:15 p.m.–5:15 p.m.   Session 3: Information Cycle and Research Strategies

Friday, August 30th

2:00 p.m.–4:00 p.m.   Session 4: Introduction to the Library Catalog

Tuesday, September 3rd

3:15 p.m.–5:15 p.m.   Session 5: Introduction to EBSCOHost Academic Search FullTEXT Elite

7:00 p.m.–9:00 p.m.   Session 6: Introduction to FirstSearch®

Thursday, September 5th

3:15 p.m.–5:15 p.m.   Session 7: Introduction to the World Wide Web

Friday, September 6th

2:00 p.m.–4:00 p.m.   Session 8: Evaluation of Information

RAINBOW BOOK

TABLE OF CONTENTS

SECTION 6 - NAVIGATING LIBROS
> Script: Navigating LIBROS
> LIBROS On-line Catalog: Finding Books, Periodicals and Government
> > Information
> Navigating LIBROS Lesson
> Sample Book Record

SECTION 7 - SURFING LIBROS
> Script: Surfing LIBROS
> Magazine and Journal Comparison
> Expanded Academic Index
> UnCover Periodical Index
> Surfing LIBROS: EAI and UnCover Lessons

SECTION 8 - ELECTRONIC RESOURCES
> Electronic Resources: Selected Zimmerman Library Sources

SECTION 9 - CIRT
> CIRT Computer Pod Guide
> Create a CIRT Computing Account

SECTION 10 - EXPLORING FIRSTSEARCH®
> Script: FirstSearch
> FirstSearch via UNM Gopher
> FirstSearch Databases: Fee Access
> FirstSearch Lessons
> FirstSearch Service Databases

SECTION 11 - INTERNET
> The Internet
> Netscape®
> World Wide Web: Search Engines, Robots, Crawlers, and Spiders
> World Wide Web: Selected New Mexico Sites
> World Wide Web: Lessons

SECTION 12 - CITATIONS
> Bibliographic Citations: How to Interpret Them

PRACTICE EXERCISES FOR CAMPUS LIBRARIES

1. Visit all the libraries on the UNM campus.

    Zimmerman Library
    Centennial Science and Engineering Library
    Fine Arts Library
    Parish Memorial Business Library
    Health Sciences Center Library
    Law Library

2. During your visit to each library, draw a simple map identifying the following services within each library:

    Circulation or Access Services area
    Reference Desk points
    Reserve Desk
    Photocopying areas
    Computerized Searching areas
    Periodical/Microform area
    Book Stacks
    Informational Handouts
    Interlibrary Loan office
    Restrooms
    Study Rooms
    Public Telephones
    Personnel Offices

PRACTICE EXERCISES FOR WINDOWS®

1. Start the computer by turning on the power strip.

2. Shut down the computer: from the Start menu, select Shut Down ... a screen will prompt you when it is safe to turn off the computer.

3. Start Button displays the following commands:

Programs	- displays programs you can start
Documents	- displays documents you have previously opened
Settings	- customizes the PC
Find	- finds files or folders
Help	- learns about Windows®
Shut Down	- properly turns off the computer

4. Application screen

   Practice: minimizing the screen, maximizing the screen, and restoring the screen.

   Close an application: Click on the box with an X in it or click on File and select Exit.

5. Toolbar

   Practice using the command shortcuts

6. Copy and Paste Functions

   Practice cutting and pasting text from one document to another.

7. Recycle Bin

   Drag text to the recycle bin and empty trash.

8. Printers

   Practice printing and using the print setup options.

9. Background/Screen Saver

   Make a screen saver that promotes Library Strategies. Select a background or wallpaper of your choosing.

PRACTICE EXERCISES FOR NETSCAPE®

1. Point and click on the Toolbar button

Back:	to go to the previous Web page
Forward:	to go to the next Web page
Home:	return to UNM General Library home page
Reload:	reload and display the current page
Print:	prints current document
Stop:	stops downloading current Web page

2. Pull down menus

    File
    Edit
    View
    Go
    Communicator
    Help

3. E-mailing and Printing Web pages

4. Downloading

    File menu, Save As, File Name, select Drive A:, save file type as HTML, Plain Text, or All files.

PRACTICE EXERCISES FOR PINE®

1. PINE E-mail is your personal account to access UNM's network

2. Set up a LOGIN ID and password.

3. Sample e-mail address: student@unm.edu

   Sample password: st1421p

4. Features and functions of e-mail

   Folder Index

   Address Book

   C= compose message

   R= reply to a message

   F= forward a message

   S= save message

   D= delete message

   U= undelete message

   O= other commands

   M= main menu

   Q= quit

   ^C= cancels message

   ^X= send a message

   ^K= cut or delete a line in the message

   ^U= uncut or undelete a line in the message

   ^O= postpones sending a message and saves it

EXERCISES FOR SEARCH STRATEGIES

Search Strategy Worksheet

1. Briefly summarize your search topic:

   _____

2. Divide your topic into major concepts. Write them on the lines below, in order of importance.

3. Under each major concept list synonymous (or alternative) terms.

FIRST MAJOR CONCEPT		SECOND MAJOR CONCEPT		THIRD MAJOR CONCEPT
	And		**And**	
_____		_____		_____
or _____		_____		_____
or _____		_____		_____
or _____		_____		_____
or _____		_____		_____

PRACTICE EXERCISES FOR
LCSH AND CONTROLLED VOCABULARY

Directions: Answer the following questions using the LCSH "big red" books.

1. What is the official heading for family and television?

2. What is the heading for family folklore?

3. What is the heading for family recreation?

4. What are some headings for racial or ethnic families in the United States?

5. What is the heading for "White" families?

6. What terms are not used for family-owned business enterprises?

7. What is a broader term for family day care?

8. What is a related term for family allowances?

9. What term is used for family counseling?

10. What terms are narrower than family psychotherapy?

EXERCISES FOR LIBROS THE ON-LINE CATALOG

Part I.

1. Search for books by Rudolfo Anaya. Limit the results of your search to books that are in Japanese. Copy the location and call number of one of the books.

2. Search for books about (i.e., on the subject of) the author, Leslie Silko. Limit the results of your search to books that are located in the Fine Arts Library. Copy the location and call number and the book's current status.

3. Search for a book on the subject of intercultural communication that was written by Roberts. Copy the title of the book, location, and call number.

4. Search for the periodical title *Journal of Social Policy*. What is the first volume of this title that the UNM General Library owns? Copy the date and issue number.

5. Search for books about business in Taos or Espanola. Copy the year of the publication for the book that is in English.

Part II.

Using the LCSH index on-line in LIBROS, answer the following questions. All of your searches will be under the SUBJECT command.

1. What terms are used for homosexuals?

2. What term is used to search for people with physical disabilities?

3. What term would you search for to find information on the Vietnam War?

4. What are some related terms for the Caldecott medal?

5. What term do you use to search for information about WIPP?

EXERCISES FOR EBSCOhost ACADEMIC SEARCH ELITE

Part I.

1. Describe the contents of this database.

2. What limit options are available? And what is the symbol for truncation?

3. Explain the difference between a Keyword search and a Natural Language search.

4. When would it be applicable to use the Browse Journal option?

5. How is a phrase like New Mexico, searchable in this database?

Part II.

1. Do a keyword search on women and capital punishment. Limit the search to peer reviewed articles? List how many were found.

2. Devise a natural language search asking about capital punishment for women. How many articles are peer reviewed?

3. Find a short story written by Leslie Silko. What is the name of the story?

4. Find an article in *Human Rights Quarterly* on capital punishment. Write down the date of publication and volume/issue number.

5. Is the fulltext of this article available on EBSCOhost? Where can you get a copy of this issue at UNM?

EXERCISES FOR FIRSTSEARCH

Part I.

Directions: For each of the searches listed below provide the following documentation for each question. Provide the name of the database or databases searched. Provide a citation or citations that answer the search and e-mail the citations to your account. Then from your e-mail account forward the citations to the LITC.

1. Find three books on the Inca Indians. Limit the search to the English language.

2. Find a citation for a copy of the Unabomber's manifesto.

3. Find a full text article on gun control.

4. Find articles on travel and tourism in New Mexico.

5. Find articles on hearing impaired children and education.

6. Find a citation for the "Family and Medical Leave Act of 1993."

7. Find an article written by Linda Farr on the degradation of trichloro-ethylene.

8. Find a medical article on the effects of Retin-A and wrinkles.

9. Find a book published by Red Crane Books on uranium and Navajos.

10. Find an article in *Wired* magazine that discusses SPAM.

Part II.

Search scenarios to discuss as a group.

1. A freshmen student wants to find articles written about Wallace Stegner's *Angle of Repose*. What databases would you recommend and why?

2. A graduate student is researching terrorism in the United States. She has not narrowed her topic as yet because she wants to find out how much information is available. What search strategies would you tutor? What databases would you recommend and why?

3. A return student to the university comes back after raising a family. She has had little computer training and has never used a mouse. Her professor has assigned her to read two scholarly psychology articles. What search strategies would you tutor? What databases would you recommend and why?

EXERCISES FOR THE WORLD WIDE WEB

1. Using Yahoo!®, find and search New Mexico State University's on-line catalog for a book by Lynn Brandvold. What is the call number?

2. Using Yahoo!®, find information on the Rio Grande Nature Center. List the URL.

3. Using Yahoo!®, find pictures of Machu Picchu in Peru. Print a copy of one picture.

4. Using AltaVista®, find a site that discusses the Greek Mythology heroes.

5. Using AltaVista®, find out where Dean Schlattmann is ranked in the PRCA Saddle Bronc competition for 1999.

6. Using AltaVista's® advanced search engine, find how to order a copy of William Adolphe Bouguereau's "Childhood Idyll" from the Denver Art Museum.

7. Using a search engine of your choice, search for a site that contains a collection of Shakespeare's sonnets in full text.

8. Using a search engine of your choice, search for a home page for the car or truck you've always wanted.

9. Using a search engine of your choice, search for the sounds of different bird calls.

10. Using a search engine of your choice, find information on your favorite movie.

EXERCISES FOR CRITICAL EVALUATION
OF INFORMATION

Part I. Popular-vs.-Scholarly Publications

Directions: Compare two periodicals, *Southwest Art* and *Art Bulletin*, and answer the following questions.

1. Describe the general appearance and format of both periodicals.

2. What is the purpose of each publication?

3. Who are the intended audiences?

4. Who are the contributors/authors?

5. Can you tell where the authors got their information? Are citations of other works consulted or researched given?

6. Can you detect any bias?

7. How timely is the information?

8. What can you tell about the financial structure of the publications?

9. Are the articles written with technical or specialized language?

10. What type of advertising is used?

LIBRARY INSTRUCTION TUTOR CASE STUDIES

1. A graduate student is seeking information on "women's heath issues" but does not want technical or medical information. The student also wants articles that are scholarly. The LI tutor uses the Search Strategy Worksheet and has the student list her topic, relevant terms, and synonyms. The student is also queried on how much research has been done to this point, how much experience the student has had searching databases, and asks if the student wants books or journal articles. The LI tutor shows the student how to search FirstSearch® and lets the student look through the descriptions of the sixty four databases available. The student chooses Contemporary Women's Issues and Wilson Select. The LI tutor guides the student through the search commands and advanced searches using Boolean Logic. The student finds several relevant articles, e-mails the citations, and, feels comfortable researching on her own.

2. An undergraduate student needs help in finding articles on gun control. The LI tutor leads the student through the EBSCOhost Academic Full-TEXT Elite®. After the student has found relevant citations, the tutor asks the tutee where he should go to find out if UNM owns the journal titles he has found. The LI tutor then has the student search LIBROS® to find the call numbers and locations for the journal titles. The student reads the journal citation to determine if the article will be in paper, microfiche, or microfilm. The LI tutor then walks the student to the periodicals area and assists the student in finding the volume, issue, and actual article in the correct format. The LI tutor assists the student further if time permits and/or if the student cannot explain the process during the review of the session.

3. A student is taking a class and the professor has put the course syllabus, course readings, and assignments on the Web. The student is unfamiliar with the Web and needs to access this course but does not understand what or how to find it with just the URL. The tutor has the student sit at the computer and goes over the basic functions of Windows®. The student then opens up Netscape® and is guided by the tutor through the basic functions and commands. The tutor then has the tutee demonstrate how to search using a URL to find the course and assists the student with navigating within the course pages and printing the assignments.

Index

Academic libraries
 as teaching libraries, 11–12
 touring, 79–81, 82
 tutor training sessions about, 79–82
Administration, library, 81
Adult learners. *See also* Tutees
 philosophy of, 34–35, 45
 tutors and, 36, 39
ALA (American Library Association), 1,
 6, 9–10
AltaVista® search engine, 95
American Library Journal, first published,
 1
Americans with Disabilities Act, and
 tutoring workspaces, 61
Association of College and Research
 Libraries, 6, 12
Auraria Library (University of Colorado),
 information literacy program, 9

Bergevin, Paul, 34–35
Bibliographic instruction, importance of,
 12
Bibliographic records, 83
Binghamton University, Peer Advisory
 Library Instruction Program,
 28–29
Books, development of, 66
Boolean logic, 67, 73

Call Number location charts, 81
Campus library tutor training sessions,
 79–82
CAPS (Center for Academic Program
 Support, UNM). *See also* Learning
 centers
 LI User Survey, 111
 LITP program structure and, 101–2
 tutor recruitment by, 105–6
 tutor training by, 104, 106–7
CAS (Council for Advancement of
 Standards), 26
Catalog departments, 54, 80, 89–90
CD-ROMs, searches using, 67
Center for Academic Program Support.
 See CAPS
Certification, tutor, 26–27, 51, 116
Circulation departments, 54, 80, 81
Classroom libraries, development of, 2
Codices, development of, 66
College Reading and Learning Association.
 See CRLA
Columbia College, library school of, 2
Communication skills, for tutors, 39–40, 68
Computer accounts, 83–85
Computer literacy, 9, 59, 120–21
Computers
 development of, 67
 and information literacy, 8–9
 within reference departments, 80
 and secondary school LITPs, 116
 and tutor workspaces, 109–10